Things that go Bump in the Night

Exploring the Haunted Heartland

Larry Wilson

ACKNOWLEDGEMENTS

To my family, friends, and colleagues for their patience during the completion of the writing of this book. A special thank you to those who shared their haunting experiences and to those allowing me to investigate their property, for the chance to experience the strangeness myself.

Contents

Illinois

Iowa

Kansas

Kentucky

Missouri

DEDICATION

This book is dedicated to my wife Kathy and son Cory. To all who have experienced the strangeness the supernatural and the unexplained have to offer. To my colleagues looking for answers to the mysterious and spectacular questions that the paranormal presents us.

Illinois

NORB ANDY'S
SPRINGFIELD, ILLINOIS

ONE

Located at 501 East Capitol Street in the middle of the commercial section of downtown Springfield, sits a two-story, rectangular shaped, brick house. Those who are acquainted with the historical side of Springfield, refer to it as the Virgil Hickox House, named for original owner Virgil Hickox. Others more familiar with the night life of Springfield, it is better known as Norb Andy's Tabarin, named after the pubs founder and longtime owner, Norbert Anderson.

But history and nightlife are not all that 501 East Capitol Street is known for. To many, like me, it is simply known as haunted!

Virgil Hickox, a man with an extensive resume, built the house in 1839. A Springfield merchant and investor, he lived in the house until his death in 1880. Originally from New York State, Hickox moved to St. Louis, Missouri in 1928. After serving an apprenticeship, he worked as a journeyman carpenter until 1833 at which time he moved to the small Northern Illinois town of Galena, working in the lead mining industry.

It was in May of 1834 that Hickox moved to the capital city of Springfield, opening a general store located directly behind where the current building stands. In addition to owning a general store, Hickox was involved in banking, the railroad industry, and politics. He served as the Chairman of the Democratic Party for many years having close ties with friend and presidential candidate Stephen A. Douglas.

After the passing of Hickox in 1880, the building built its own resume, some of which is on the morbid side. In 1895, the building became the location for the Sangamo Club, an exclusive men's club that was located at 501 East Capitol until 1911. Branson's Funeral Parlor moved into the building in 1916 and remained there until 1926.

It was during the 1918 Spanish flu epidemic that the basement of the funeral parlor was used as the overflow to the county morgue. As the story goes, people were dying so fast from the deadly virus, when someone died, their bodies were removed from the victims home and transported to the funeral parlor, deposited down a shoot located on the west side of the building, where the bodies remained until they could be prepared for burial.

At one point during the epidemic, bodies in the basement overflow were stacked from floor to ceiling. It is rumored that some of the bodies brought to the morgue were not dead, but merely in a comatose state, later to be found alive.

From 1927 to 1938, the building housed several businesses including a flower shop, and a combination sandwich shop and tavern called Cude's-Beer Stube. The most well know business to occupy the basement level of the building is Norb Andy's Tabarin, a nautical themed bar that includes a collection of knots used in sailing displayed above the fireplace.

Norbert "Norb" Anderson, founded the business in 1939 and ran it for some forty years. Subsequent owners have re-opened and closed the establishment since the days of Anderson. Unfortunately, most have been short lived, lasting only a matter of months. It was during one of the short-lived reopening's of the tavern, that I was allowed access for my most recent investigations.

The investigations took place on October 23, 2016, and Halloween night the same year, when the tavern reopened under the ownership of partners Dave Ridenour and Todd Gedaminski.

Between 2007 and 2012, I investigated the building on three occasions. All were somewhat uneventful, however, this would not be the case during the 2016 investigations, as the pub had a few tricks of the paranormal kind up its sleeve.

My decision to conduct a fourth investigation at Norb Andy's, stemmed from a simple trip past the old building after work one afternoon. Capitol Avenue was not the shortest route home for me, but several times per month, I would take a detour on my way home, just to drive by the haunted landmark. I guess you could say, I am a bit obsessed when it comes to the paranormal, and locations like Norb Andy's attract me, like a magnet attracts steel. I had driven by the building many times since my last investigation, each time thinking, what a shame such a beautiful landmark sat empty.

Virgil Hickox House-Norb Andy's

One afternoon was different when I drove by. I noticed a sign near the entrance of the bar, indicating that it was open for business. So, I decided to stop by and strike up a conversation with the bartender, hoping he or she would be receptive to talking about the haunted reputation of the building. Plus, there is nothing I like better than talking about ghost while consuming a few pints of cold brew.

When entering the establishment, the first thing you notice is the nautical theme of the bar. Particularly noticeable is a large ships wheel and framed collection of seaman's knots, hanging on the wall. The dim lighting adds to the cozy appearance and atmosphere of the pub. Norb's has always reminded me of Cheers, the bar from the television series of the same name.

When I walked in, the place was deserted except for a young female bartender who greeted me. I took a seat at the bar, and we exchanged pleasantries. She introduced herself as Sarah and asked what I would like to drink. For those who are curious, I ordered a tall Coors Light.

Wasting little time getting to my reason for stopping in, I handed Sarah my business card. I asked her if she knew the bar had a reputation of being haunted, which she did. I explained to her that I had investigated the bar and adjoining Hickox House several times under the previous owners. Then proceeded to ask her if she had experienced anything unusual during her time working at the bar. Her expression was enough to answer my question, but she verbally responded as well.

"Yes," she replied. "As a matter of fact, I had something weird happen just a few days ago. Plus, I know that Todd, one of the owners, has had several strange things happen to him in recent weeks."

"What did you experience?" I asked.

"Well," she said. "I was working behind the bar like I am now, when one of the employees brought a stack of freshly *laundered towels and placed them on the bar for me to fold and put away. I was busy with a customer, so momentarily, I turned my back to finish serving them. When I turned around, I was shocked, because all the towels were neatly folded and stacked next to where I was working. No one was nearby and I turned away for only a few moments. There wasn't enough time to fold and stack the towels in the short time my back was turned. It was freaky! Stranger yet,"* she continued, *"the towels were soaking wet and were dry when they were placed there."*

When Sarah finished her story, I confessed that the actual reason I stopped in, was to talk to the owners to see if they would allow me to do an investigation some night. I explained my background as a private investigator and the length of time I had been investigating the paranormal. Sarah said she was sure the owners would be receptive to an investigation, since both had experienced unusual activity and openly talked about their encounters.

"As a matter of fact," Sarah said. *"Dave, one of the partners will be here shortly, so you can ask him for yourself."*

While we chatted, a customer came in and sat at the bar a couple of stools down from me. Sarah was occupied with the customer, when a tall thin man walked in and sat down directly across the bar from me. He was friendly, and we exchanged greetings from across the bar.

Call it fate or synchronicity, but no sooner than we exchanged pleasantries, the man began talking about an odd experience he had in the adjacent Hickox House portion of the building earlier that day. I couldn't believe what I was hearing. It was like he was reading my mind. Based on what he said, I assumed he was Dave the owner who Sarah had mentioned. He began our conversation by asking if I knew the building was haunted.

"Actually," I said. *"You won't believe this, but that's the*

reason I stopped in this afternoon." "Is that right," he said with a surprised but interested look on his face. With that, I grabbed my beer and seized the opportunity by taking a seat next to him on the opposite side of the bar. After shaking hands, I introduced myself and handed him my business card. I gave Dave a brief rundown on my background and explained I had investigated the building on several occasions and wanted to talk to someone about doing another investigation.

"Well, you are speaking to the right man," he said. *"I'm Dave Ridenour owner of the building."* After introducing himself, Dave continued with the story he started to tell a few minutes before.

Earlier in the day, Dave and another gentleman were painting at the top of the stairs in the Hickox House. They had been working several hours and nothing seemed out of the ordinary. Then discernible movement caught Dave's attention causing him to turn and look.

When he did, he saw a dark, shadowy mass, moving along the wall near the doorway. Shocked at what he was seeing, Dave turned toward the other gentleman, who was looking at Dave. *"Did you see that,"* the man asked Dave. *"I saw something,"* Dave replied.

The two compared notes and agreed what they saw looked like a person moving about the upstairs. *"Darndest thing I ever saw,"* Dave said with a half grin, half puzzled look on his face. *"I knew the reputation of the place, but never expected to see anything like that."*

Upon accepting Dave's generous offer of a beer on the house, our conversation continued. He was curious about what I do as a paranormal investigator. I explained my background and experience as both a private and paranormal investigator, then gave the Cliffs Notes version of how I conduct my investigations and gather evidence. Several minutes into our conversation, I figured it was time to asked

Dave for permission to investigate. He was receptive to the idea, with the stipulation I also get permission from his business partner and co-owner Todd Gedaminski, to which I agreed to do.

Dave told me that Todd was gone for the evening but would be in the following day doing renovation work in the Hickox House. *"You should ask Todd about some of the weird things that he has experienced recently,"* Dave added. *"He's seen some really crazy stuff around here!"*

The following day, I returned to the bar on my lunch hour to talk to Todd as Dave had suggested. It was shortly after 1:00 p.m. when I arrived, so the lunch crowd had thinned out a bit. I asked a female employee working behind the bar if Todd was around. She pointed to the rear of the bar where a tall man wearing a baseball cap and yellow shirt was standing.

Wasting no time, I walked to the rear of the bar and introduced myself and explained the purpose for my visit. I told Todd about the conversation I had the night before with Dave and asked if he had a few minutes to discuss the strange things he had experienced in the building. *"Sure,"* he said laughing." *But you'll probably think I'm off my rocker."*

I reassured Todd that I had seen enough crazy things over the years, that nothing he told me would make me think that he is crazy. He began by explaining that before he became involved with Norb Andy's, he never gave any thought to ghost or the paranormal and had never really formed an opinion as to whether such things existed. *"But I'm a total believer now,"* he said. *"You have to believe it because there's no other explanation for it. It's what we deal with here at Norb Andy's on a daily basis."*

Todd explained that he is a carpenter by trade and had been doing extensive remodeling work on the Hickox House portion of the building for several months. *"For ninety-six days I worked long hours in the building and never saw or experienced anything unusual. Then one morning that all changed,"* Todd said.

"I came in early to have coffee before I started work for the day. It was early, somewhere around eight o'clock. The only other person in the building, was a guy who was doing some computer technology work for us. We were seated at that table," Todd said, pointing to a table directly across from the bar. *"We were talking and drinking our coffee when something behind the bar caught my attention. When I looked up, I saw this little blonde-haired girl running behind the bar toward the kitchen. She had long flowing curly blonde hair and was running and playing like she didn't know or care that we were here."*

I asked Todd if she looked solid or more like an apparition. *"She just looked like a little girl running and playing and then disappeared into the kitchen."* Todd went on to explain that the man, who was with him, must have seen his head and eyes following the little girl as she ran, because he looked at Todd and said, *"You just saw something didn't you,"* to which Todd replied, *"You wouldn't believe it if I told you."*

His second experience happened under similar circumstances, once again while having morning coffee with the man at the same table. Todd had his back to the front door and was looking toward the gaming room at the rear of the bar. The room had been used to drain the bodily fluids from corpses being prepared for burial when the building housed the overflow to the City Morgue.

Pointing toward the back room, Todd began his story. *"We were sitting and having coffee, when I saw something move at the back of the building. I looked up and saw this tall shadowy silhouette of a man standing in the doorway of the gaming room,* Todd explained.

"He caught me totally by surprise. He was just standing in the doorway looking in our direction. It startled me, this

ghost or whatever the heck it was, was huge! I turned toward the other guy, got his attention, and asked him if he wanted to see a ghost? But before I had a chance to show him, he looked up and pointed toward the rear of the bar and said, you mean the guy standing over there? He saw him too!"

Continuing, Todd said, *"I couldn't make out any facial features of the ghost, he was just this black silhouette of a man, and he was huge. You couldn't miss him; he was as tall as the doorway."*

We walked toward the backroom as Todd continued describing what he saw. At 6 feet 4 inches tall, Todd is well above average in height. As he stood in the doorway of the room to show me how tall the figure was, I noticed that the top of Todd's head was a couple of inches below the top of the doorframe. This meant that the shadowy figure was at a minimum, 6 feet 6 inches tall.

Not long after Todd witnessed the phantom girl and the shadow man, he had a third encounter, also in the bar area. The incident took place during the daytime while customers were in the bar.

"I was standing in the dining area with a white bar towel slung over my shoulder," Todd began. *"From behind, I felt someone put his or her fingers on my right shoulder and press down hard. Enough force was applied that it pushed my shoulder down several inches. Thinking that it was one of the staff playing a prank, I turned around to see who was messing with me. When I did, no one was there. It was one of the craziest things I have ever had happen to me,"* Todd said, shaking his head. *"Physically being touched and feeling the fingers of a hand pulling your shoulder down, makes you a believer pretty quick,"* he added.

Todd told of a more recent incident that occurred a few days prior to my interview with him. He had been working the entire morning in the upstairs portion of the building, cutting wood trim, with a heavy commercial grade circular saw. Deciding to break for lunch, he unplugged the saw, wound the cord up and placed the saw on top of an upside-down plastic milk crate. Locking the door behind him, he left the upstairs portion of the building, headed downstairs, and entered the bar from the Capitol Street entrance.

When he walked down the steps and into the bar, one of the restaurant staff greeted him with a surprised look on her face. She questioned Todd by asking, *"What the heck are you doing up there?"* *"What do you mean,"* Todd replied.

"Well, just before you walked through the door, there were several loud crashes that came from upstairs."

Based on the timing of when the girl heard the noise, Todd realized he would have already left the upstairs and locked the front door, so, it wasn't him that caused the noise. Curious, he decided to head back upstairs to see if he could figure out what she heard.

The first place Todd checked was the area he had been working. To his surprise, he noticed the heavy commercial grade saw he left a top the milk crate, was now positioned on the opposite side of the room from where he left it.

"There is no way the heavy saw could fall off of the crate and end up all the way across the room," Todd exclaimed. *"It's simply too heavy. Even if I placed it too close to the edge of the crate and it fell off due to gravity, it could not roll across the room on its own. Plus, if it fell off the crate, there would have been damage to the floor, like a gouge or scratch, but there was no damage whatsoever."*

If hearing Todd's accounts of seeing the ghost girl, the shadow man, phantom fingers touching him and a heavy commercial grade saw mysteriously move on its own wasn't enough to get my attention, he had one more experience to tell me about. It would be an experience I would see repeat itself in a mere ten days, during my Halloween night investigation.

Todd began his story by having me follow him to a jukebox, located on a wall adjacent to the bar. He explained that in order to power the unit on or off, you must use a remote control, which is kept on a shelf located behind the bar. The unit has two speakers, one located at the front of the bar and the other located at the rear of the dining area. The volume level for each speaker can only be adjusted by using the remote control.

"The maximum we set the volume to, is level thirty, and we do so only when there is a large crowd. Otherwise, we keep the level set at ten," Todd explained.

"Several times our chef has told me when he arrived in the morning, the jukebox was blasting away. It was not that I didn't believe him; I knew that for the unit to be powered on, someone has to have access to the remote," he continued

One morning after closing the bar the night before, it happened to Todd. *"I couldn't believe it!"* he said. *"I know I powered it off the night before and walked out in silence. But when I came in that morning, the music was blasting so loud, I couldn't stand it. The volume for both speakers were set to level one hundred. It was the darndest thing I had ever seen,"* Todd explained, shaking his head.

After Todd finished telling me about his encounters with the paranormal at Norb Andy's, our conversation turned to discussing the particulars of scheduling an investigation and without hesitation, Todd agreed to allow the investigation.

Whether due to the construction, having customers and employees in the bar again or both, something stirred up the activity taking place. I knew from experience, the sooner I conducted the investigation, the better the chance I had to experience activity as well. Because it seems that paranormal activity runs in cycles where either a great deal of activity occurs or none at all.

Investigation
Friday October 21, 2016

I arrived at Norb Andy's at 9:30 p.m. Todd was behind the bar and was talking to an attractive strawberry blonde, seated at the bar. I later found out this was his girlfriend, Terri. Working alongside Todd was a female bartender, serving a drink to a man, who at the time was the only customer. I remember thinking to myself, that a downtown tavern in the capital city, only having one patron on a Friday night, was not a good sign for business. On the other hand, it was good for my investigation, since it would not take long to clear the bar after it closed.

I greeted Todd, then unveiled my plan of action for the night. Since the bar was still open, I would not be able to investigate the basement until the bar closed for the night. The Hickox House portion of the building was not in use, so I sat up my audio and video recording equipment there first, then when the bar closed, would set up equipment in the basement.

From my earlier investigations I knew that routine conversation from the bar does not interfere with audio recordings in the upstairs portion of the building. So, at 10 o'clock, I headed upstairs to begin the investigation.

Todd accompanied me and unlocked the outside entrance at the front of the building, because there is no direct access from the bar to the upstairs. After he did a quick walk through with me, he returned to the bar.

I placed audio recorders throughout the building. Three in rooms on the second floor and three more in various rooms on the first floor. One recorder was placed in a room on the first floor, with a newly constructed bar. I point out this room because several high-quality EVP's were recorded in the room.

I spent time in each room during the early portion of the investigation, which lasted from 10:00 p.m. to 1:30 a.m.

11:45 p.m.
I was on the first floor, in the room with the bar, and was seated on a bar stool, listening for unusual sounds or movement. One advantage of investigating alone in total darkness, is it enhances your sense of hearing, enabling you to hear subtle sounds that might be missed, with the lights on or if accompanied by someone.

I had been sitting on the bar stool for a few minutes, when suddenly, I was overcome with the feeling I was being watched. Then without warning, I heard a loud bang come from the next room. It sounded like someone slammed a window shut.

When we conducted the walk-through, I didn't notice any open windows, so a window slamming shut, didn't make sense. Plus, it was October and chilly outside. If a window were open, I should have felt a draft caused by cold air coming in.

I called out, *"Is anyone here? If so, make that noise again."* It was at this point; I started to get a weird vibe and felt a sudden change in the environment. I no longer felt I was alone.

Still seated on the bar stool, I listened for additional sounds. There was nothing at first, then a loud noise came from the second floor. It sounded like someone pulled down a window shade and released it, causing it to recoil to the top of the window.

With flashlight and video camera in hand, I headed upstairs to see if I could figure out what had caused the noise. Unfortunately, due to the clutter from years of storing unused items in the upstairs rooms, I couldn't determine what caused the noise or where it came from. I walked around the upstairs listening for additional sounds, but heard nothing, so I headed downstairs and reclaimed my seat on the barstool. Shortly after midnight I conducted the only EVP session of the night.

For those who are not familiar with the term, EVP, it is the acronym for *"Electronic Voice Phenomena,"* which are voices and sounds recorded by audio and video equipment, sometimes heard when recorded while other times they are not. Paranormal enthusiasts have various theories as to what the voices are, including, disembodied voices of the dead, interdimensional beings, time travelers and demons to name a few.

During EVP sessions, I verbally provide ground rules for the session. For example, I will say something like, *"If there are any spirits or beings present, please answer my questions by speaking aloud. This way, I will be able to physically hear what you have to say, or my recording devices will record your answer and I will be able to hear your response later."*

Of course, unless a voice or sound is physically heard after asking a question, I won't know if a response was made until I return home and review the recorded audio. On this night, the later was the case, as I recorded several sounds and one clear voice that seemed to be a direct response to a question I asked.

A few days later while reviewing audio from my recorder I had placed near the bar on the first floor of the Hickox House, I found a response to one of my questions. It was recorded shortly after midnight, during the EVP session, after I asked the following questions. *"Were you married? What was your wife or husbands name?"*

When I asked the questions, the only sounds I heard, were the whistle of a nearby train, and a sliding sound, caused by my foot that was on the floor while seated on the barstool. In the recording, you hear my foot make a sliding sound, followed by a male voice that whispers, *"Nicole."*

Was the voice a spirit saying a random name or was it answering my question and telling me that he was married to someone named Nicole? Whatever the case, it shows an intelligence was present, and heard my question. In my opinion, the timing of the answer is too precise to be coincidence. In addition to the voice whispering, *"Nicole"*, I recorded the banging sound, I heard earlier coming from the upstairs.

Another compelling piece of evidence was recorded shortly after the Nicole response. I recorded what sounds like someone snapping their fingers, immediately followed by human sounding whistling. It was as though someone or something, were trying to get my attention or were curious to see if I could hear the sounds they were making, which I did not.

The time was approaching 1:30 a.m., and all was quiet in the Hickox House. The bar closed at 1:00 a.m., so I headed downstairs to set up additional recorders. When I entered the bar, Todd, the female bartender, and Teri, were having a conversation as all the customers were gone for the night. Todd asked how things had gone upstairs, so I gave a brief rundown, explaining the noises I heard.

After my conversation with Todd, I set up additional audio recorders. One across from the bar, one near the jukebox, and one in the backroom where Todd witnessed the shadowy figure in the doorway. I placed a video camera equipped with infrared capabilities at the front of the bar. Once the equipment was set up, I joined Todd, Terri and the bartender further explaining the noises I heard upstairs.

During the conversation, the bartender told me how she feels uncomfortable when upstairs. She said, she has never seen or experienced anything to cause the feeling, but it is overwhelming for her.

At 2:00 a.m., the bartender decided to leave for the night. Since it was late, Todd escorted her to her car. It was while Todd was walking the bartender to her car that Terri and I witnessed something we could not explain.

We were seated at the corner of the bar with our backs to the front door, having a conversation, when suddenly, the wall by the kitchen door, lit up in a bright orange glow.

The glowing light, lasted three or four seconds, then vanished. All the lights were off, so the glowing light was clearly visible to us. We turned and looked at each other, both asking at the same time, *"Did you see that?"* Getting up from my seat I hurried to the other side of the bar. I didn't see anything that could have caused the glowing light. We compared notes and concluded we both saw the same thing, a glowing orange light.

When Todd returned, we told him what we saw, and he knew of nothing in the bar that would cause such a light. Unfortunately, the remainder of the night was uneventful, so, at 4:45 a.m., I packed up my equipment and ended the investigation.

As I drove down Route 29 heading home, I reflected on the events that took place. Nothing earth shattering had occurred, I thought to myself. I heard a couple of unusual sounds, but after all, it is an old, cluttered building. The glowing orange light was harder to explain away, as I didn't have a logical explanation for what caused it.

I wasn't disappointed by the lack of activity during the investigation, because over the years, I have found that it is usually the uneventful nights, when the best audio evidence is recorded. As it turned out, I recorded the *"Nicole,"* EVP which seemed to be a direct response to my question and I also recorded the snapping and whistling sounds, both of which, were good evidence. But little did I know while driving home, that in only nine days, I would get another chance to investigate the building, and this time, it would really show me what it could do!

Wednesday October 26, I received a Facebook message from local television personality Lindsey Hess. In her message, she asked me to call her and provided her telephone number so that I could do so. She indicated that she wanted to do a story related to the paranormal to be aired on local television station, FOX 55 for Halloween. So, after work, I called Lindsey from my car to get further details about what the focus of her story would be. She told me that she had been discussing the possibility of doing a segment on the paranormal with her friend and colleague Chris Neal, who works behind the scenes at the station in the production department.

It was Chris who suggested she contact me. Lindsey went on to explain that I knew Chris but knew him by another name. As it turned out, I did know Chris through his other profession, as a local radio personality. Chris is better known as Jammer, working for Springfield radio station, 99.7 KISS FM, which is now 99.7 THE MIX.

I had been a frequent guest discussing my paranormal adventures; on KISS FM's Morning Grind radio show hosted by another radio personality and friend Bondsy. It was during one of my appearances that I met Chris. So now the connection to Chris made sense.

Lindsey explained that what she wanted to do, was tag along with me on an investigation at a place believed to be haunted and record the investigation. She would present the results of what we found and her experience on their Halloween broadcast. The only night Lindsey had available to do this was Sunday night October 30th, which was only four nights away.

I explained I would be happy to take her somewhere, but our main obstacle would be time. By this I meant, that after investigating, it takes time to review all the raw audio and video that is recorded, to see if any evidence has been obtained. Conducting the investigation, the night before the broadcast, would not allow enough time to do this.

Since we would not have enough time to review the evidence, I presented another option to Lindsey. I told her about my recent investigation at Norb Andy's and the audio evidence I recorded, including the *"Nicole"* EVP and the snapping and whistling sounds.

The option I presented to Lindsey was to investigate Norb Andy's, so she and her cameraman could experience what a paranormal investigation is like, and since there would not be enough time to review the audio and video from the investigation before her broadcast, I would allow Lindsey to use the *"Nicole and snapping and whistling"* EVP's recorded during the first investigation, for the newscast.

In the meantime, I contacted Dave and Todd to get their permission to do the investigation, and to see if they would be willing to go on camera with Lindsey, to talk about the ghostly activity they witnessed. Permission was granted and both agreed to interviews.

Investigation
Sunday October 30, 2016

On Sunday evening, October 30, I arrived at Norb Andy's at 6:30 p.m., the pre-arranged time Todd and Dave had agreed to meet me.

The bar closed at 6 o'clock, so there would be no noise distractions from customers to contend with during the investigation. Lindsey was scheduled to arrive at 7 o'clock. to interview Todd and Dave. When finished, she would head back to the studio to anchor the 9 o'clock news broadcast, then return to Norb Andy's at 10 o'clock to begin the investigation. While waiting for Lindsey to arrive, I played the audio clips from the previous Friday night's investigation for the owners, and both were amazed at the clarity of the whispery voice saying, *"Nicole!"* Neither knew of a connection between the name or anyone associated with the bar or building named Nicole. Historical research I conducted did not turn up a connection either. Being the home of the former county morgue, there are many names connected to the building, that historical records would not reflect.

At 7 o'clock, Lindsey arrived. With her, was a cameraman and her colleague and friend, Chris Neale. After exchanging pleasantries, Lindsey conducted the interviews with Dave and Todd. When she finished, we went over the game plan for the night, which included placing audio and video recorders throughout the building, conducting several EVP sessions, and staking out the place, in anticipation of catching a glimpse of the strange activity that takes place.

Staking out a building, is the same basic method of investigating I used when conducting surveillances as a private investigator. So basically, I sit tight and wait to see what unfolds. It is amazing what one can hear when sitting quietly in the shadows of a darkened building or secluded location.

After explaining the plan for the night, it was time for Lindsey to head back to the station to prepare for her 9 o'clock newscast. While the television crew was away, I placed audio and video recorders throughout the building. I chose locations where unexplained sounds and voices were experienced during the previous investigation, as well as areas where Todd and Dave had experienced activity.

When Lindsay and Jammer returned shortly after 10 o'clock, all the equipment was in place. I could see by the enthusiasm and excitement in their voices, they were looking forward to spending the night in a haunted building. As is the case for most who are about to embark on their first paranormal investigation, I could see a bit of apprehension to go along with their excitement. I see this when taking someone with me who has never been on a paranormal investigation before. Their eyes scan the shadows looking for someone or something that may or may not be there, as the feeling they are being watched becomes overwhelming, half expecting an unseen hand will reach out and grab them.

The investigative team for the night would consists of Todd, Lindsey, Jammer, and me. Dave would not be part of the team, as he left after his interview with Lindsey. We began our adventure in the Hickox House. The bar and the house have separate entrances, so each time we moved our investigation from the bar to the house or the house to the bar, Todd locked the door behind us, so no one else had access to that part of the building. You will see the importance of this information, later in the chapter.

We turned all the lights off and used flashlights to find our way around. I thought it best if the four of us remained together during the investigation, so when I reviewed the audio, it would be easier to determine if something said was one of the team, or the disembodied voice of a ghost.

Early on, the investigation was uneventful, or so it seemed. Because it was not until a few days later when reviewing recorded audio, I discovered we had activity going on right under our noses, as several clear EVPs were recorded. But I am jumping the gun a bit, as the EVP's will be discussed later in the chapter.

During the investigation, two unexplained events occurred, including a cool but creepy event that took place at exactly, 4:03 a.m. It is an experience the investigative team will talk about for years to come.

The first unexplained activity, occurred a few minutes before 2:00 a.m. We were in the hallway on the east side of the Hickox House. Todd was several feet away, facing Lindsey, Jammer, and me. Our flashlights were off, so it was completely dark. Todd was re-telling the story about being grabbed by his shoulder while working in the bar. Suddenly, I heard what sounded like a woman talking. The voice came from the south or directly behind the group.

Immediately I asked, *"Did anyone just hear a voice coming from behind us?"* To which, both Lindsey and Jammer replied, *"I did!"* Todd, who was talking when the voice spoke, said, *"I didn't hear anything."* It was agreed that the voice was female and was only a few feet behind us. We couldn't hear what was said, because the voice spoke while Todd was telling his story.

Unfortunately, as many times is the case during paranormal investigations, even though the voice was loud enough for us to hear, it was not recorded by our audio recording devices. However, we did record two female voices in the Hickox House during our investigation, which I will discuss a bit later.

We investigated the house for another hour, but never heard the voice again. Since all was quiet, we decided to lock up and move next door to the basement tavern to continue the investigation. Little did we realize, in less than an hour, we would witness an event, that none of us will ever forget.

Since the tavern portion of the building is relatively small, we did a short walkthrough of the backroom and the east hall storage area, then camped out at the bar. Lindsey, Jammer, and I were seated at the northwest corner of the bar, with Lindsey to my left, and Jammer to my right. Todd was behind the bar and leaning on it with his forearms. After discussing some of the peculiar things that Todd had witnessed since becoming associated with the tavern, we decided to do what I call, *"quiet time."*

Quiet time is like conducting a stakeout for unexplained noises and voices. Then if something is seen or heard by one of the team members, we investigate, and try to find the source of the activity. Before we started quiet time, I commented to Jammer, how it felt like someone was watching us from the doorway at the south end of the room, to which he agreed.

All the lights were off, so the bar was very dark. As I turned my head toward the left, in the direction of Lindsey, something caught my eye in the obscure lighting. I saw a powder blue light, reflect on the wall just behind her. It was like the orange glow I saw the week before that came out of nowhere.

Before I could say anything, a pinkish light, reflected off Todd, who was still standing behind the bar in front of me. Next, a bright yellow light lit up the bar area, illuminating the entire investigative team.

At first, I could not tell where the source of the light was coming from, then in an excited voice, Jammer said, *"Look, the jukebox is turning on!"* Simultaneously the group turned to the right and looked. Sure enough, the jukebox had powered on all by itself. The pastel colors I had seen reflecting on the wall, were coming from the now brightly lit jukebox. Then, without warning, a song began to play.

When the days are cold
And the cards all fold
And the saints we see
Are all made of gold
When your dreams all fail
And the ones we hail
Are the worst of all
And the blood runs stale
I want to hide the truth
I want to shelter you
But with the beast inside
There's nowhere we can hide
No matter what we breed
We still are made of greed

This is my kingdom come
This is my kingdom come
When you feel my heat
Look into my eyes
Its where my demons hide
Its where my demons hide
Don't get too close
Its dark inside
Its where my demons hide
Its where my demons hide

The song? *"Demons"*, by the group, Imagine Dragons.

The jukebox is an iTunes juke box that can play thousands of music selections. So, what are the odds of this song, playing in a haunted bar being investigated for ghosts? My guess is, astronomical!

Do I think that a demon or some type of malevolent spirit played this song to scare us? No, not at all. But I do believe that one of the spirits or beings that haunts Norb Andy's, has a sense of humor.

A few days after witnessing the juke box turning on by itself and playing its own selection of music, I researched iTunes jukeboxes and how they work. Although, playlist can be programmed using any cell phone having the model and serial numbers of the jukebox, one thing they cannot be programmed to do, is turn the machines on or off. To do this, the remote for the unit, must be used.

The night we witnessed the jukebox playing on its own, the remote was stored on top the refrigerator behind the bar and no one was anywhere near it. What we saw, validated the experiences of Todd and his cook, who found the jukebox playing several times when they arrived for work in the morning. Unfortunately, the battery for the camera I had pointed in the direction of the jukebox ran down before the box began to play. But there were four eyewitnesses who saw it.

The ghost of Norb Andy's must have saved its best trick for last, as nothing else was experienced by the team the remainder of the night. I was scheduled to appear on a morning radio show for Halloween at 6:00 a.m., so we began breaking down the equipment at 5 o'clock, and called it a night.

Lindsey and Jammer were lucky. Because it is rare for someone tagging along on their first investigation to be fortunate enough to witness something strange like a jukebox playing on its own. Not to mention they heard a disembodied voice as well, which will make a believer out of you that ghostly things exist.

During the investigation, EVP's were recorded as early as 8:38 p.m. and as late as 2:55 a.m., in the Hickox House. When they were recorded, no one was in that part of the building. Nothing was recorded in the bar area.

A couple of the recordings have me shaking my head a bit. I would place them in the category of the bizarre, when compared to most EVPs I have recorded over the years. As I mentioned, when the 8:38 p.m., EVP was recorded, no one was in that part of the building, and the only entrance, was locked.

The best way to describe what we recorded; is it sounds like a witch laughing. The type of laugh you would expect a cartoon character to make during a children's Saturday morning cartoon show. The laugh is a loud and clear, *"Ha-ha-haaa!"* The last part of the laugh has emphasis on it and is drawn out. It is totally bizarre.

A second and equally bizarre voice was recorded shortly after 11:00 p.m. You will recall that during the October 21st investigation, I heard what sounded like a window slamming shut, but when I searched for an open window, there weren't any. During the October 30th investigation, the team and I were discussing the sound of the window slamming that I heard during my first investigation. As a result of the conversation, we decided to try and recreate what I heard.

To do so, Todd opened a window that was only a few feet from where I had been standing the night I heard the noise. He tried to recreate the sound, by forcibly slamming the window shut. When he did, it sounded nothing like what I heard and recorded on the 21st.

Upon reviewing the audio, I discovered that during Todd's re-creation, as soon as he slammed the window shut, the voice of a female child can be heard singing. The lyrics of her brief song are both chilling and unnerving because the voice sings, *"You're going to hell."*

The rhythm and lyrics of the short tune are reminiscent of something you would hear in a Stephen King movie. Although conjecture on my part, based on the timing of the voice and Todd shutting the window. I wonder if she was shaming Todd for closing the window or shaming us for looking for ghost?

The next disembodied voice was recorded at 2:50 a.m. It was recorded after we left the Hickox House and Todd had locked the door. I place the recording in the category of bizarre, due to the sequence of events that can be heard before and after the voice speaks.

First, you hear the sound of two footsteps, that abruptly stop. As soon as the footsteps stop, a male voice calls out *"Danielle."* Next, there is a squeak that sounds like the hinge on a door, followed by the sound of a door shutting, then silence.

It wasn't until after I played the recording for Lindsey and Jammer, that I found out from Lindsey, that she had a close family member who had been tragically killed years ago. The name of her loved one, was Danielle. Of course, there is no way to know if the Danielle that the voice refers to, has a connection to Lindsey's deceased family member or if it is simply coincidence. With the number of bodies brought to the building when it was the overflow to the County morgue, it is possible that a lost soul was looking for another Danielle who passed and was taken to the building.

Another clear EVP was recorded only five minutes after the Danielle EVP was recorded. At 2:55 a.m., a female voice says, *"Come close."* The voice is beckoning someone to move closer, but since none of us were in the Hickox House at the time, I assume none of us were being summoned.

Mysterious bangs and phantom voices heard coming out of the darkness. A jukebox powering on by itself, playing a song titled, *"Demons."* Footsteps, doors closing, and a name called out by a disembodied voice that were all recorded. These are the type of things you would expect to find in a haunted location, and as you have just read, we did.

If experiences like this are not enough to convince one that a location is haunted, then I am not sure what will. I know what Lindsey and Jammer experienced, made believers out of them, that the paranormal is real.

Just as Todd said to me the first time I met him. *""You have to believe it because there's no other explanation for it."*

Well, I agree with you Todd, and it is places like Norb Andy's that keep me coming back for more and make investigating the paranormal worthwhile.

THE LEGACY THEATRE
SPRINGFIELD, ILLINOIS

TWO

Sometimes you can feel that a place you are investigating, is haunted as soon as you walk in the front door. I'm not psychic, but when entering such a place, my sixth sense, a sense that we all possess, seems to kick in. The type of place I refer to, is not necessarily spooky, but has a feel to it that someone or something is lurking in the shadows. The environment is different. It's a feeling that a presence from the past still lingers. As you venture about, you feel eyes watching your every movement.

Over the last two decades, I have found this type of place to be varietal gold mines for recording disembodied voices. Springfield, Illinois Legacy Theatre at 101 East Lawrence Street, is the type of place I refer to.

Located in the heart of Illinois, Springfield serves as the hub of the state's political activity. The city became the state capital in 1839 with the help of a young lawyer named Abraham Lincoln, who lived in Springfield until 1861, when he left to become the 16th President of the United States. Many believe that citizens from days gone by, still roam the streets and buildings of Springfield, appearing out of nowhere to haunt those whose paths they cross.

The quaint and friendly atmosphere of the theater gives the feeling that you have taken a step back in time and perhaps when you enter the building, you do. The Springfield Theatre Center, as it was originally called, was the venue used to showcase live performances for the Springfield Theatre Guild. On November 8th, 1951, the theatre opened its doors with a performance of the Broadway show Born Yesterday. After the opening the business received congratulatory telegrams from famous celebrities, such as Bob Hope, Bing Crosby, and Broderick Crawford.

One of the members of the Theatre Guild was actor Joe Neville. According to some, Joe was odd and at times arrogant. Some cast and crew members did not like him. In addition to his arrogance, Joe had a mysterious side as well. It was rumored that he previously acted in England under a different name, but being a talented and dedicated performer, his past was overlooked by his fellow actors.

In 1955, Joe was given the lead role in the play, Mr. Barry's Etchings and all was well, or so one would think. Unfortunately, things were not as they seemed. After a dress rehearsal for the opening of the play, Joe returned home and committed suicide, overdosing on pills, never performing in the show.

It was determined the reason Joe ended his life was due to an audit at his place of employment. Funds had been misappropriated and Joe was the likely suspect. But as they say, the show must go on, and his role was assigned to another actor one day before the show was set to open.

Today, some who frequent the Legacy believe Joe's spirit still lingers inside the theater. Reports of paranormal activity began almost immediately following Joe's death and continue to this day. Actors and stage crew have reported strange sounds, such as doors opening and closing on their own, lights turning on and off without reason, and costumes and tools disappearing that are later found folded or placed in an area which had been previously searched. Some claim they have seen Joe's spirit wandering the Theatre Center. Most of the sightings occur prior to the opening of a new show.

Today, the Theatre Center has a new owner and a new name, The Legacy Theater. Owner Scott Richardson has started a new era as he greets the faces of fresh guests who come to be entertained. But not all the entertainment takes place on the stage. Strange encounters have led some to believe that spirits from the past continue to linger, refusing to move on to their final resting place, preferring to remain and frequent the quaint and friendly atmosphere of the Legacy. Owner Scott Richardson has experienced some of the strange phenomena that occurs on a regular basis, firsthand.

I met Scott in early June 2011, just weeks after he purchased the old theater. I had been trying to get into the Theatre Center for months but was unable to find the right person to authorize an investigation. Fortunately, my good friend Lynn Puls, a local hairstylist and owner of The Hair Shanty, was asked to help style wigs for a play taking place that July at The Legacy. Although Lynn had never met Scott before, he asked her to meet with him to discuss hairstyles for the play. During the meeting with Scott, Lynn mentioned that her friend, Larry Wilson, was interested in conducting a paranormal investigation of the theater. She asked Scott if he knew who to contact to allow access to the building for an investigation and Scott replied, *"As of a few days ago, me!"*

The first week of June I met up with Scott and he gave me a ninety-minute tour of the theater. During the tour, he described some of the strange occurrences that he had encountered since becoming owner of the building.

When Scott was considering purchasing the theater, he went on several walkthroughs of the building. During each of the visits, he noticed that the building gave off a depressed or negative feeling. But the first time he walked in the door after taking over as the new owner, he noticed it had a completely different vibe. It had a feeling of relief, as if the building knew that it was about to get a face lift and soon would come alive again with performances and spectators.

The theater sat idle for several years and needed a lot of work to get it in condition to once again host performances. There was so much to do that Scott was not sure what needed to be done first. Finally, he decided to start with the landscaping, to give the outside a fresh look.

Stage and Auditorium

Perplexed at where to begin, he contacted a local landscaper and arranged to meet with them the following day. *"I locked the building before going home for the evening and took the only key with me,"* Scott explained. *"The next morning, when I unlocked the door and entered the building, I found the original building plans, rolled up on my worktable. They were not just any plans; they were the original landscaping plans."* Scott said that he had been through all the paperwork that was left in the building, and the original plans for the exterior, were not included with the paperwork. *"No one, but me, had access to the building. Where the plans came from, is still a mystery,"* Scott explained. This, however, was only the beginning of strange things to come.

One day, Scott was doing repair work on the stage using a hot glue gun. *"I laid the glue gun down next to me and turned away for just a split second*, Scott Said. *"When I turned back, the gun was gone and was nowhere to be found. Later, I was getting ready to leave for the night when I noticed something behind the last row of seats in the auditorium. Underneath a seat, with the cord neatly wrapped around it, was the glue gun. To this day, I have no idea how it got there,"* Scott said shaking his head.

Another evening, Scott was alone in the building when he heard what sounded like someone taking a handful of nails and throwing them in the air on the stage. *"I heard the pinging sound of nails landing on the stage, but when I checked it out, nothing was there."*

Investigation
June 17, 2011

On June 17th, 2011, I investigated the Legacy for the first time. Accompanying me was a paranormal enthusiast named Jay, who was on his first investigation. During the investigation, a few showers and thunderstorms moved through the area which added a spooky atmosphere to the night.

We arrived at the Legacy at 7 o'clock with Scott arriving a short time later. Scott decided to stay for a while and do some spackling work to prepare walls for painting. As he went about his business, Jay and I did a walkthrough of the building, recording baseline temperature and electromagnetic field (EMF) readings.

Many paranormal investigators believe fluctuations in EMF, is a by-product of the presence of spirits. Unfortunately, homes and buildings like the Legacy have a lot of electrical wires running in walls and underneath floors, which cause fluctuations in EMF, making the data unreliable in the detection of ghost and supernatural beings. For this reason, I don't spend a lot of time monitoring electromagnetic field readings. However, monitoring temperature is a different story. I have more faith in the use of temperature fluctuations in ghost detection, as I have personally experienced extreme temperature variations at haunted locations. During the Legacy Theatre investigation, the temperature remained at seventy-five degrees upstairs and slightly cooler in the basement.

Scott left at 9:00 p.m., so Jay and I set up video cameras and strategically placed digital audio recorders throughout the building. For the most part, the night was quiet, and neither of us had any personal paranormal experiences. However, around 11:00 p.m., I was standing in the doorway of an old dressing room in the basement that Joe Neville may have used at one time. Jay was in the dressing room conducting an EVP session. Suddenly, I felt someone or something tickling my back. My first thought was that something ghostly was touching me, but when I turned around, I discovered a bat was fluttering on my back!

As the night progressed, we were disappointed in the lack of activity. After all, a place with the reputation of the Legacy tends to get your hopes up. At 4:00 a.m., we completed our investigation and began to break down our gear. Even though the night was uneventful, we had hours and hours of recorded audio and video to go through, so we hoped our time and effort would be fruitful. As it turned out, it was. Because upon reviewing the evidence, I found audio which confirmed we were not alone during the investigation, and had company, other than a pesky bat!

One of the strangest EVPs sounded like someone speaking with a foreign accent. When it was recorded, Jay and I were having a conversation about the investigation. Although Jay's heritage is from India, he was born and raised in central Illinois, and does not have an Indian accent. During our conversation, after Jay speaks; you hear a loud and clear voice with an Indian accent say, what I first thought sounded like, *"Creloza."* We didn't know what it meant or if it was possibly a person's name. I talked to people of Indian descent to see if they were familiar with the word, and they were not. We also used online language converters without success. The clip remained a mystery until recently.

I do a weekly paranormal podcast called, *"The Paranormal Pursuit,"* with Jason Bond, better known as "Bondsy," who is the morning show host on Springfield radio station 99.7 The Mix. On season one, episode ten, Bondsy and I discussed my investigations at the Legacy Theatre, and I played the aforementioned EVP. Immediately Bondsy spoke up and said, *"I don't think it is saying, Creloza, it's saying, Close-up, only with a strong Indian accent."* After listening to the EVP a few more times to get the speech pattern down, I clearly heard what Bondsy was hearing. So, the voice with the Indian accent, wasn't saying Creloza after all, but was saying "close-up," which would make sense, in a theatre setting.

The next EVP is one of my all-time favorite EVP's I have recorded. We were in the basement near what was once the concession area. I had placed a digital recorder near a door on a folding metal chair. Unexpectedly, a sump-pump turned on in a nearby room, causing a loud noise. Realizing the sound from the pump would create a noise problem for our audio recorders, I decided to close the door to muffle the sound. To do so, I had to move an extension cord that was draped over the top of the door, to close it. I had a video camera in my hand, so I laid it on the chair next to the audio recorder and shut the door. As I shut the door, the sump pump turned off.

When I reviewed the audio from the recorder on the chair, I found I had recorded a voice that seemed to be talking to me. In the audio clip, as soon as I close the door and the sump pump turns off, a clear male voice whispers, *"You left shit there,"* as if to remind me that I had left my equipment on the chair. The recording is one of the clearest EVPs I have recorded over the years. If the voice was interacting with me, then it knew I was there, making it an intelligent spirit or haunting. In case you are not familiar with the terms intelligent spirit or intelligent haunting. An intelligent spirit or haunting is when an entity interacts with the living, having an intellectual awareness about it.

The next EVP also seemed to be of an intelligent origin. The voice sounds exactly like the voice who declared, *"You left shit there."* When the EVP was recorded, Jay and I were having a conversation about our disappointment with the lack of activity during the investigation. In the recording, you hear me say, *"It's really calmed down out there,"* referring to the thunderstorm that had moved out of the area. To which Jay jokingly replies, *"Well, at least we experienced the bat flying around,"* referring to the bat that had bumped my shoulder. Immediately after I say, *"It's really calmed down out there,"* a clear, whispery, male voice says, *"That's your own conclusion."* So, I guess the spirit had a difference of opinion!

Two compelling EVPs of singing were recorded forty-five minutes apart. The singing was not just ordinary singing but sounded like a man and a woman rehearsing for a performance. It is simply amazing.

Even though the June 2011 investigation didn't produce personal experiences, modern technology allowed us to capture evidence, proving an invisible world although not seen with the naked eye, exists, nonetheless.

The audio evidence offered proof that paranormal activity is taking place at the Legacy and gives credence to the stories that have been told for years.

Later that same year, I conducted a second investigation, in which the physical manipulation of a light switch was witnessed.

Investigation
October 31, 2011

The June investigation may have lacked personal interaction with the ghost of the Legacy, but Halloween night of the same year would offer the type of unexplained interaction that causes a twenty-two-year investigator to scratch his head. The incident I refer to, involved a motion sensing security light in the basement.

Jay accompanied me on the investigation along with three paranormal colleagues and investigators named Jamie, Chris, and Tim. Tim was along on the investigation to use specialized equipment called MESA which stands for Multi-frequency Energy Sensor Array. His equipment, collects data on a variety of energies associated with hauntings, including, infrared, visible and ultraviolet light intensities, natural and artificially generated electromagnetic fields, gamma ray, radiation, galvanic skin response of a human subject, infrasound, and vibration. Tim also deploys still and video cameras as well as audio recorders to document paranormal phenomena. If you would like to find out more about MESA, you can do an intranet search using the key words, "MESA Project and Tim Harte."

Unfortunately for Tim on this night, he would miss an incredible paranormal experience, as he was monitoring his equipment on the stage area while the unexplained interaction I am about to tell you, took place.

The remarkable incident stemmed from a motion sensor light in the basement that was interfering with an infrared camera we were using in the old dressing room area. The light from the security system was a problem because it caused an overexposure for the infrared camera which is designed to film in the dark. Even though we found the switch for the security light, no matter if we turned it to the off position, it would not go out. We even turned it off and left the area figuring if it is controlled by a motion sensor, our movement may cause it to stay on. But when we came back to the area it was still on.

Investigator Jamie had to leave early, which left Jay, Chris and I in the basement and Tim monitoring his equipment upstairs on the stage.

Figuring that turning the light off was a lost cause, we continued our investigation in the basement with the light on. We decided to conduct an SB-7 Spirit Box session, in hopes that our audio recorders would record responses made by disembodied voices.

For those not familiar with the SB-7 Spirit Box and how it works, the device is a mini-AM-FM frequency sweeper, which is an altered radio that is fine-tuned to scan AM or FM radio frequencies. It scans forward or backwards, at a rate measured in milliseconds. The scan-lock mechanism on the radio is disabled, therefore, the device continuously scans radio frequencies at a predetermined rate. Sort of like twisting the knob on a radio backwards and forwards quickly, to produce random noise.

The original device was invented by amateur radio enthusiast Frank Sumption, who read an article about recording EVP that appeared in Popular Electronics magazine. Sumption built a radio receiver he believed allowed real-time communication between the living and the dead and entities from other dimensions.

At first, I didn't buy into the box working. I believed the sounds coming through were nothing more than radio static or skip coming through, along with a phenomenon known as audio pareidolia. Audio pareidolia is the process of our mind, trying to make sense out of unfamiliar sounds and words and correlate what we hear, to familiar words and sounds.

I changed my mind, when I noticed how particular words coming through the box were answers to specific questions I asked. In addition, at the rate I scanned the frequencies, which is one-hundred milliseconds per second, whole words and complete sentences should not be coming through when they are being vocalized by the same voice. Our box session was conducted just outside of what was once Joe Neville's dressing room. The session started off slow, with an occasional audible voice coming through, but nothing that was pertinent to the questions we were asking.

After twenty minutes or so, the voices coming through, were suddenly clearer and louder. At one point I asked, *"Is Joe Neville present?"* Immediately, we heard a voice say, *"Joe."* Of course, we couldn't tell if the voice was saying that it was Joe or if it was a questioning voice asking, *"Joe who?"*

Thinking to myself, *"If this is Joe Neville and he is here in the building, maybe we can get some type of response to confirm it is him."* So, I said, *"If Joe Neville or any spirits are present, can you please turn off the light, because it is interfering with my video camera."*

As soon as I asked the question, the lights went out! *"That's not possible,"* I thought to myself. So, I said, *"Thank you,"* and asked, *"Can you please turn the lights back on again for us?"* Without delay, the lights immediately came back on. We looked at each other dumbfounded. Even though he was standing three feet from the light switch, I asked Chris, *"Did you flip the switch?"* To which he replied in an excited voice, *"No, I'm nowhere near it!"*

Hoping the third time would be a charm, I said, *"Just one more time, can you turn the lights off again please?"* Instantly the lights went out. This was unbelievable. We had tried every means possible to turn the lights off without success. Now all I had to do was asked and they would go on or off. Someone or something invisible, was manipulating the lights.

Even though I had already said, *"Just one more time,"* when the lights turned off the second time. I decided to push the envelope and ask the presence to manipulate the lights, to see what would happen. So, I said, *"Just one more time, can you please turn the lights back on again?"* No sooner than I spoke, the lights turned on, but instantly turn off, then back on, then off again. This on and off sequence continued for close to a minute. The lights turned on and off so fast, it would be impossible to flip the switch at that pace. They were basically flickering like a strobe light. It was as if who or whatever was manipulating the lights were saying, *"Ok wise guys, I can turn the lights on and off all night, but what's the point?"* If I had not been there to personally witness what happened with my own eyes, I would not have believed it.

The next morning, I called Scott Richardson and asked him if this had ever happened before. He explained that not only had this never happened, the way the lighting system is set up, it wasn't possible. If this was the case, then who, or what was manipulating the light switch? Was it Joe Neville, or another spirit from days gone by who still roams the theatre? I will probably never know the answer to my question, but the experience is one that ranks high on the list of the things I have witnessed as a paranormal investigator and one I will never forget.

The next time you pass by the Legacy Theater at 101 East Lawrence Ave in Springfield, stop by and take in one of the performances. Feel free to strike up a conversation with one of the friendly patrons, but if you feel a cold chill and the hair begins to stand up on the back of your neck, you may want to take a second glance at the person sitting next to you, just in case!

ANDERSON CEMETERY
PALMER ILLINOIS

THREE

A chilling incident occurred early on in my paranormal investigating endeavors. It took place at a rural cemetery in Christian County Illinois, in 2007. The experience made a believer out of this former private investigator, who was trained to base conclusions on logic and tangible evidence, that ghost are real and yes, they do roam graveyards.

Located near the small town of Palmer, Illinois is Anderson Cemetery, or as some call it, Graveyard X. The graveyard has been widely discussed by paranormal investigators and curious locals for years. It is a place most prefer to steer clear of at night. Strange sounds and voices of small children playing have been heard in the cemetery. Unexplained floating lights have been seen both during the daytime and at night. Anomalies appear in photos and digital thermometers record icy cold temperatures in warm weather, with no scientific or logical explanation for the temperature fluctuations. I personally experienced an extreme temperature drop at Anderson, which you will read about shortly.

To keep the location from others, books and internet postings labeled the cemetery, Graveyard X. This created a false perception that Anderson was a secret location. In 2007, the stories and legends about the mysterious graveyard, piqued my interest enough to compel me to find it, and conduct my own investigation into the legends and lore.

Finding Graveyard X was my first challenge, because all I knew about its whereabouts was that it was in a secluded place, in rural, central Illinois. Fortunately, I uncovered a paranormal message board on the internet and found a posting requesting directions to the cemetery. A member of the message board, posted a response, listing the latitude and longitude for Anderson Cemetery in central Illinois. I entered the coordinates in a Google search and found a site that listed cemetery locations. Unfortunately, the coordinates were for another Anderson Cemetery located in the same county. Using the same message board, I eventually found directions to the correct Anderson Cemetery.

As it turns out, Anderson, or Graveyard X, is in rural Christian County only nine and a half miles from my home in Taylorville. So, it was right under my nose all the time. So much for the intuition of a former private investigator!

My initial trip to Graveyard X, was made during the daytime to make it easier to find and map out for a return trip to investigate at night. Sunday, March 4, was a clear day, with a temperature around thirty degrees and a slight breeze. To my surprise the graveyard was not the creepy, eerie place I expected. Instead, it was pleasant and well maintained. However, on my next investigation, I would find out firsthand, that once the sun goes down, it's not so pleasant.

Anderson is three miles from the nearest town, Palmer, Illinois. From Palmer, I headed north on Fifth Street, then traveled down a country road until coming to a green sign with an arrow directing travelers to the cemetery. Turning left at the sign, I followed a narrow winding road for another mile and there it was, the elusive mysterious graveyard I had heard and read so much about.

I wandered about the cemetery conducting a pre-investigation, mapping out the grounds, taking photos, and using a digital voice recorder to see if I could record anything unusual. Unfortunately, nothing eventful happened. The only activity I saw were several flocks of wild geese and a bald eagle flying overhead. I took fifty to sixty photos hoping to capture a ghostly image, but only two of the photos had anomalies in them.

In the photos, a prism or rainbow color appeared. They were taken at high noon, so the sun was directly overhead. The rainbow effect may have been nothing more than glare or a reflection, but it puzzled me why the distortion only appeared in the two photos.

As far as I know, I don't have psychic abilities, but I had a strange feeling that something was there, and it was laughing at me, as if to say, *"Sorry, nothing is going to happen this afternoon, but come back at night and I will show you what I can do."*

After finishing the pre-investigation, I planned to return

Graveyard X

the following Thursday, to see what the graveyard had to offer at night. I wanted to see if the tales and legends that made this place so mysterious were true. Well, we should be careful what we wish for, because soon, I would get more than I bargained for and experience what the forces at Anderson had to offer.

On Tuesday, March 6, I arranged with a close friend, who was also interested in the paranormal, to accompany me on Thursday nights investigation. The plan was to arrive around 6:00 p.m., which would allow enough daylight to set up equipment and get a feel for the surroundings before darkness set in. I knew once the sun set, the natural sounds of the wooded area surrounding the cemetery, would sound mysterious and creepy. Hopefully, getting familiar with the sounds of the location before dark, would alleviate misinterpreting ordinary sounds for something paranormal.

As luck would have it, Thursday morning my friend informed me he would not be able to go on the investigation, which meant for the first time, I would be investigating a secluded cemetery at night, and I did not relish the thought of being alone in a place with the reputation of Graveyard X.

At 5:30 p.m., I loaded my equipment and began the nearly ten-mile trek to the site. For some reason, I kept thinking about the old Don Knotts' movie, The Ghost and Mr. Chicken, in which a mild mannered, wannabe newspaper reporter spends the night alone in a haunted house. The movie is one of my all-time favorites, and I felt much like the Don Knotts' character, Luther Heggs, who had cold feet at the thought of spending the night alone in a haunted mansion.

Although, this would be my first experience investigating a cemetery alone at night, it would not be my last, as I have done this many times since. Over the last ten years, I primarily investigate hauntings alone, investigating the full gamut from secluded cemeteries, haunted houses and even several former funeral homes by myself. As a matter of fact, I now prefer investigating alone.

When I arrived at Anderson, the sun was starting to set, and shadows were becoming more apparent. I unpacked my equipment and began the short walk from the parking lot to the cemetery. I had no apprehension about the place, nor did it feel creepy. Birds were chirping and there was a peaceful calm that gave a false sense of security about the place. This, however, would soon change.

One book I read, claimed the most active area in the cemetery, was in the oldest part of the graveyard at the north end. The boundaries of the area described, were marked by a stone bench under a large oak tree, a tall monument, and a gravestone in the shape of an arch forming the graveyards own Bermuda Triangle of sorts. I located the area during the pre-investigation and decided to concentrate my Thursday night investigation in this area.

The large oak tree was full of chirping black birds when I arrived. It reminded me of a scene out of the Alfred Hitchcock thriller, "The Birds." Even though the chirping was annoying, it offered a sense of comfort, because if the birds were not on edge, why should I be. A few minutes later, just before sun set, the birds suddenly stopped chirping. It was like someone flipped a switch and turned off the sound, and they knew something else was there besides me.

Not only did the birds stop chirping, the slight breeze that had been blowing, stopped as well. There was no movement of any kind in the surrounding woods. As darkness set in, the graveyard had a different feel to it, and the once peaceful feeling, turned to a feeling that I was being watched. Sort of a, calm before the storm feeling.

Forty-five minutes passed, and it was now pitch black in the graveyard. I walked the perimeter of the triangulated area, looking and listening for anything out of the ordinary. For several minutes, I stood in the same spot near my video camera, with my arms folded and a camera hanging from my neck. From what I read, if I were going to experience ghostly activity, it would take place in this part of the cemetery. From the vantage point where I was standing, I had a good perspective of the entire area. Everything was quiet, when suddenly, I heard the sound of footsteps just a few feet in front of me, and to my left. When I heard them, I looked up expecting to see someone coming toward me, but no one was there.

It sounded like a person scurrying about. The grass was still crisp and frozen from the cold winter, so I could hear the crunching of grass as the footsteps scurried about. Then, without warning, the footsteps walk past me. I could feel the breeze caused by who or whatever it was. It was the type of breeze you feel when someone passes you in a hallway or on a sidewalk. I not only heard them; I felt the presence of whatever it was, as it passed by, but saw no one.

I knew they were there, but they were invisible. Pretending like I had not heard anything, I slowly turned around, and took a photo with my camera. I reviewed the photo, but all that was in the picture were a few tombstones.

Even though the temperature was in the low thirties, my forehead was sweating like I was in a sauna, and I was shaking like a leaf. I stood quietly listening for the footsteps and any movement.

After fifteen or twenty seconds of chilling silence, I heard them coming again. Like before, they passed to my left. It was the same scurrying or shuffling sound. Once again, I felt the breeze as it passed by. The hair stood up on the back of my neck, as I turned and attempted to take another photo. Unfortunately, the digital display of the camera flashed low battery, and the flash failed, so no picture.

The low battery message was puzzling, because I had just installed new batteries before arriving for the investigation. Although, it could have been caused by the cold temperature affecting the battery charge, after using the camera flash when I took the first photo.

Again, I stood motionless listening for movement, thinking

that who or whatever was there, was in front of me. As I stood there, hands trembling, listening, and facing toward the east, without warning, someone, or something, with great force, struck me in the middle of my back. The blow felt like a closed fist. But that was impossible because no one was there. The punch was so hard, it caused me to lose my balance and stumble forward. I was wearing a t-shirt, sweatshirt, and winter jacket that was unzipped halfway. My jacket was puffed out in the back but when the punch landed, it hit hard enough that it pressed the jacket against my back.

An instant chill went down my spine and I could hear and feel my heart pounding in my chest. It felt like someone was standing to my left, so I attempted to take a photo, but again, the flash failed. Standing still and in shock, I listened for movement, wondering what would happen next, but nothing did.

I stood motionless a bit longer, then walked around the area for another five to ten minutes, when a sudden, empty feeling came over me. Thinking to myself, *"Hey, you are all alone in a remote, secluded cemetery, and were punched by something you can't see and have no idea what its intensions are. Is it playing with you, trying to scare you or is it telling you, it's time to move along?"* Since discretion can be the better part of valor, I decided to pack it up and call it a night.

Even though I had heard the rumors and read the stories about Graveyard X, I came to Anderson Cemetery with a healthy mix of skepticism and an open mind. But never in my wildest dreams did I expect to be punched by a ghostly entity.

What happened was the type of experience I read about as a child, but never expected to experience for myself. Whatever punched me, quickly made a believer out of me, that the stories and rumors about Anderson Cemetery were true, and ghost are real. My experience was firsthand, so there was no denying the place was haunted.

In October of the same year, I returned to Graveyard X with paranormal investigator Ed Osborne. Ed was a very knowledgeable paranormal investigator and someone I had a great deal of respect for. It was the Wednesday night before Halloween and was a cool, but not overly cold evening.

Ed and I had been in the cemetery for close to an hour, taking pictures, checking for electro-magnetic field readings, and monitoring temperature levels. Nothing seemed to be out of the ordinary. The time was approaching 7:30 p.m. and the curfew for the cemetery was 8:00 p.m. Since the county sheriff's department patrolled the cemetery, we decided to make a final pass through, and leave by curfew.

As we were making our final pass, I scanned the graveyard to check the temperature, using a digital laser-pointed thermometer. Everywhere I scanned, the temperature reading fluctuated between forty-three and forty-four degrees with the average temperature at forty-four degrees Fahrenheit. The readings remained consistent until I passed by the cement bench under the oak tree.

As I neared the bench, the temperature began to rapidly drop. First it dropped below forty degrees Fahrenheit, then below thirty degrees, then twenty degrees. The temperature continued to steadily drop until it finally reached a low of minus sixteen degrees below zero. This happened in less than a minute. Neither Ed nor I could believe what we were seeing. To confirm there was not some type of equipment malfunction, or that the thermometer was set to Celsius instead of Fahrenheit. I shut the device off, turned it back on and reset it to Fahrenheit.

When I re-scanned the cemetery, just as before; the average reading was forty-four degrees everywhere I checked. Everywhere that is, except the spot next to the concrete bench, which was still below zero.

My hands were uncomfortably cold, and my nose felt like it

was becoming frostbitten. Whenever I moved the thermometer more than four or five inches from the cold spot, the temperature would go back up to forty-four degrees. But as soon as I moved it back, it would register below zero.

At 8:15 p.m., we decided to leave since it was after curfew, and we were trying to be respectful of the cemetery rules. The temperature was still minus eleven degrees Fahrenheit in the spot next to the concrete bench, when we left the graveyard. My fingers and nose were so cold, when we got to my vehicle, I had to turn the heat on to warm them up, because they felt like they were frozen. Based on an average temperature of forty-four degrees, at one point, we experienced a sixty-degree temperature drop, which did not make sense.

I have been back to the cemetery many times since and have never recorded such an extreme temperature fluctuation again. Ed and I continued to investigate together from time to time and without fail, the subject of the cold spot would come up. It was a mind-boggling experience and one that left a lasting impression on us. Sadly, Ed passed away a few years ago, and is greatly missed.

Several years after experiencing the extreme temperature drop, I met longtime paranormal investigator Tim Harte, who I consider a friend and respect as a paranormal colleague. During one chat, our conversation turned to Anderson Cemetery. Unbeknownst to me, Tim was part of an investigation and filming of a documentary at Anderson several years before my investigation.

As he was explaining some of the unusual phenomena that his team experienced, he mentioned an extreme temperature drop, that was recorded by three team members at the same time. *"It was crazy,"* Tim said. *"We recorded a temperature of thirteen degrees Fahrenheit in July, on an eighty-nine-degree day. The temperature was recorded using three different recording devices."*

I told Tim about the extreme temperature readings that Ed and I recorded in 2007. Tim had not told me where they recorded the readings in the cemetery, so when I told him we recorded the below zero readings in front of the concrete bench by the large oak tree, his eyes grew wide. Because this is where they recorded the cold temperature as well.

Anderson Cemetery more than lived up to its reputation for me, because as it turned out, the rumors of the place being haunted were not rumors at all but were haunting fact. The footsteps and punch in the back were my first ah-ha moment as a paranormal investigator, that proved to me, ghosts exist, and yes, they really do roam cemeteries.

GRANITE CITY YMCA

FOUR

Who's watching
Tell me, who's watching
Who's watching me
- Pop Artist, Rockwell

Many times, when I hear a particular song on the radio it reminds me of experiences I have had on investigations. When I hear the lyrics from the 1984 song, *Somebody's Watching Me*, by Rockwell, I immediately think of the July 2013 investigation I conducted at the old Granite City YMCA in Granite City, Illinois. Not only was some unseen force watching us that night, it, or they, physically interacted with us, by throwing objects at us as well.

Granite City is located in Madison County, Illinois, just seven miles on the eastern side of the St. Louis metropolitan area. The city was founded in 1896. However, the area itself was settled much earlier than the official founding date of the community. Prior to becoming a city, the area was settled by the French, followed by German and English settlers. Due to its proximity to the Mississippi River, Granite City prospered during the explosion of the Industrial Revolution. Locals Frederick and William Niedringhaus founded the St. Louis Stamping Company, which later became Granite City Steel.

In the early 1800s, settlers began to farm the fertile lands to the east of St. Louis, and in the 1830s, the area became known as Six Mile, due to the distance the area was located from St. Louis. In 1896, Granite City incorporated as a city and became part of Madison County.

Due to the plentiful jobs created by the Niedringhaus brothers, the city grew in population. The name, St. Louis Stamping Company was changed to the National Enameling and Stamping Company, in hopes of attracting a wider customer base. As the company prospered, it not only succeeded in attracting a wider customer base, but the appeal of plentiful, well-paying jobs, attracted many European immigrants, from Macedonia, Hungary, and Bulgaria, who were in search of a better way of life in America.

Many of the immigrants settled in an area west of downtown that would later be called, Hungry Hollow. Several tragedies occurred in this area of town, with the first being the flood of 1903 that covered all of what is now the western part of Granite City. I have heard stories that during the great flood some of the immigrants who were living in tents drown, and their bodies were never found. However, I must go on record by saying, I have not been able to confirm or document the story. As a result of a lack of jobs, many of the immigrants went without food, and unfortunately, some starved to death.

On August 28th, 1924, ground was broken, and the cornerstone for the Granite City YMCA was laid on May 11th, 1925. From information I found, the YMCA was officially opened sometime around January 3rd, 1926. In 1954, a viewing area and wing, which housed racket ball courts, was added to the existing structure. In their early years, Kevin Cronin, and the popular band, REO Speedwagon, performed a concert in the YMCA gymnasium.

The YMCA is located in a primarily commercial neighborhood at 2001 Edison Ave. The building sits in the same area of town where tragedy struck the immigrants in the early twentieth century. Unfortunately, much like the land that the building occupies, sources I spoke to, alleged that the YMCA has had its own share of tragedy since opening.

Reports of deaths, both in and outside of the building, have been rumored over the years. One such claim is a young girl, between the ages of nine and twelve years old, drowned in the swimming pool while playing with other children. Other deaths include the murder of a man on the front steps of the building by a 14-year-old boy, during a failed robbery attempt. A former janitor, who was mentally challenged, allegedly hung himself in a small work area, near the old locker rooms. As the story goes, the man was smitten with a female member of the YMCA who shunned him. Broken hearted, he hung himself.

Two other male members died from heart attacks on the premises. One in the men's locker room and another man named, Andrew, died while watching a movie in the dayroom. He was 63 years old when he died. Sources told me of a possible death in Room 207 as well, but details on the cause of death were not known by the source. Once again, I would like to point out, I have not been able to confirm or document any of the alleged deaths in the building through records. But many times, legends and lore can be hard to confirm.

The 1111 Phenomena Strikes Again.

For those who know me or have read my books, you already know that since I started investigating the paranormal, I have been seeing repeating number sequences of 11 and 1111, quite often. So often, it's a bit freakish. It's not an occasional occurrence, but something I experience all of the time, whether it be a quick glance at a clock, or seeing the number 1111 on a license plate at exactly 11:11 a.m., while reading a text message that was received at 11:11 p.m. the night before, which happened to me several years ago. The odds for all of those things happening at the same time would have to be astronomical.

Soon after I started noticing the repeating number sequences, I also noticed an increase in synchronicities or what skeptics call coincidence in my life. But, if you know me, you know that since I began delving into the paranormal, I no longer believe in coincidence.

The following story is the reason I bring up the repeating number phenomena.

I am always looking for new locations in the Midwest to investigate, but the way I was able to gain permission to investigate the old YMCA, is a bit uncanny. While looking for new places in Illinois to investigate, I conducted a Google search using the key words: haunted and Illinois.

As I looked through the search results, I found a webpage for a paranormal group, located in Quincy, Illinois. On their webpage, was a list of locations they had investigated and a link for an investigation they conducted at the YMCA in Granite City, Illinois.

As it turned out, I knew several members of the Quincy group, through a presentation and book signing I had done for them. So, I decided to contact a member of the group, to see if they had contact information or knew who to get in touch with, to gain access to the Granite City YMCA.

Since I was busy finishing up reviewing evidence from a recent investigation, I decided to hold off contacting the Quincy folks until a later time. Meanwhile, I continued doing research on the YMCA, and found several newspaper articles about a paranormal group from Granite City who had investigated the old YMCA. One article had a phone number for an investigator named Bill, who was listed as the contact for anyone interested in investigating the building. This meant I could simply call Bill and wouldn't need to contact my Quincy friends for the information.

As I was reading the article, Bill's phone number caught my attention because it was, ###-###-1111. When I saw the 1111, I knew I was destined to investigate the place.

Several weeks went by and I still hadn't called him. I remember it was a Tuesday morning when I finally decided I would give Bill a call on my lunch hour to see if I could schedule the YMCA for an investigation. As luck would have it, a friend invited me to lunch, so I wouldn't have time to make the call, but would call him on my way home from work.

On the way home, I picked up my cell phone to call Bill and introduce myself. When I did, I noticed I had a missed call. I selected the option on my phone to display missed calls. As I read the number, I couldn't believe my eyes. It was "###-###-1111." Right away, I recognized it was Bill's phone number due to the area code and the 1111. But how and why would he be calling me, I thought to myself. To be clear, he didn't know me and as far as I knew didn't have my cell phone number.

I hit the redial and called the number. Bill answered and we exchanged a few pleasantries. I shared the eerie coincidence of how I had been planning to call him for several weeks, to try and schedule an investigation at the YMCA, and on the very day I decided to call him, he called me.

He explained that the Quincy paranormal group, who had recently investigated the building, gave him my name and phone number. He had mentioned to them that he was organizing a paranormal conference to raise funds to restore the old YMCA. When he told them he was looking for guest speakers, the group recommended he contact me.

During our conversation, Bill asked if I would be interested in speaking at their fundraising event, which I agreed to do. He asked how much I charge for speaking engagements, and I informed him I don't charge for fundraisers. Since I wasn't charging for my presentation, Bill indicated he would allow me access to the building and conduct my investigation for free. We finished our conversation with the understanding I would call him back in a few days, with the date I wanted to conduct the investigation, which I did. The date we agreed on, was Thursday, July 25th, 2013.

Bondsy, from Springfield, Illinois radio station, 99.7 KISS FM, was interested in scheduling and recording an investigation with me, for his annual October Halloween show and since Granite City was only ninety minutes away from the station, I figured it would be the perfect place. When I told him about the old YMCA, and explained the history of the building, he was all for an investigation there.

We decided to conduct the investigation from 10:00 p.m. the night of July 25th and finish up around 4:00 a.m. the morning of the 26th. Since the investigation involved the radio station, the investigative team was a bit larger than normal. It consisted of Bondsy, his co-host, Sarah Savannah, and two female interns from the station, nicknamed Trigger and Lil Beans. Neither of the interns, had been on a paranormal investigation, which always makes for an interesting night. Also joining us for the investigation was paranormal investigator Chris, who I mentioned earlier in the book.

The plan was to meet Bondsy, and his radio team in Springfield, at the station at 8:00 p.m., then we would make the almost two-hour drive and meet Chris at the YMCA building in Granite City. On my way to Springfield, to pick up the radio crew, I decided to call Bill, to make sure he knew what time we would arrive for the investigation. Eerily when I picked up my phone to dial Bill's number, my phone started to ring. When I looked at the number of the incoming call, the hair stood up on the back of my neck. Because the number the call was coming from was, ###-###-1111. It was as uncanny as the first time I made phone contact with Bill. When I saw his phone number light up on my phone, I knew the investigation would be a good one.

Bill was calling for the same reason I was preparing to call him, which was simply to confirm the time we would be arriving.

After picking up the KISS FM crew at the station, we headed south on Interstate 55 to Granite City. We arrived shortly before 10:00 p.m. Chris was waiting for us in his car, having arrived a few minutes earlier.

Leaving our equipment in our vehicles we entered the building, and were met by Bill, and several members of his team. After brief introductions, Bill, and a member of his team, gave us a tour of the building. While doing the walkthrough, similar to what I described in the chapter on the Legacy Theatre, I began getting a strange feeling when Bill took us to two locations in the building.

One was in the old locker room and pool area, and the other was on the second floor of the building. As it would turn out, before the night was over, we would have activity and excitement in both locations.

Bill took us to an area near the racket ball courts, where a great deal of old drywall had been pulled down and was in piles. He said they were trying to clean up the old building to make for a more pleasant experience for groups to conduct investigations. But the main reason he wanted to show us the demolition area, was to warn us to be careful where we walked and sat, because when they tore out the old drywall, they ran into an infestation of Brown Recluse spiders, which are poisonous and can cause serious health issues. As Bill warned us about the spiders, he aimed his flashlight at the pile of debris, where hundreds, if not thousands of the spiders were crawling around.

After witnessing the invasion of the spiders, Bill took us to the locker room and pool area and told a story about a little girl who was playing with friends and somehow drowned. Visitors to the building have claimed to hear the disembodied voice of a child in the pool area. Behind the pool, is a workroom where it is alleged a former janitor hung himself.

Next, we headed to the second floor. Bill told us that for some reason, visitors to the building, feel uncomfortable when on the second floor. It is rumored that someone died in room 207, but there is no documentation to confirm the story. As it would turn out, a short time later we would have our own experience on the second floor.

During the walkthrough, several members of our team, especially Bondsy, felt uneasy in several rooms near the staircase. As you will read, this would only be the beginning of the uneasiness for Bondsy, on this night.

When Bill finished the tour, we headed back to the first-floor lobby, where we set up our basecamp for the night. After bringing in our equipment, Bill and his crew left, and we had the building to ourselves.

The Swimming Pool Area

The Investigation

Due to the uneasy feeling team members had, we began the investigation on the second floor in the area closest to the staircase, and the strange feeling still lingered. Trigger and Lil Beans were notably anxious , so they stayed close to the group. But after all, it was their first investigation.

Nothing unusual was going on, so Lil Beans and I headed

to the racquetball courts, down the hall from the rest of the team. Bondsy, Sarah, Trigger and Chris continued exploring the rooms near the staircase.

Soon after entering the racquetball area, Lil Beans heard what sounded like faint voices. She insisted they were not the voices of the rest of the team, but unfortunately, I couldn't hear them. She heard them for several minutes, then they suddenly stopped, so we exited the racquetball courts and stood in the hallway to see if we could hear the voices. Suddenly, the raised voices of our fellow team members bellowed down the hallway. They were excited about something, so we hurried down the hall to find out what was going on.

When we met them, Bondsy looked at me and said, *"Dude, you're not going to believe what just happened!"* I could tell by the excitement in his voice, that something unexpected had occurred. Sarah was calm compared to the others, but she had been on investigations with me before.

Bondsy explained that while Chris and Trigger were checking out a room at the end of the hall, it sounded like something was thrown toward he and Sarah. They were searching for the object, but so far, no luck in finding it. He said whatever it was, bounced several times and had a hollow metallic sound to it. Sort of a ping, ping, ping sound.

I could tell by the expression on his face that Bondsy was unnerved by what had happened. Even before the object was thrown, he was on edge, and I had never seen him act this way before.

We continued searching for the object that caused the noise. Chris found an empty .22 caliber shell casing on the floor and tossed it down the hallway. Immediately the group agreed it was not the same sound. We even kicked it, in the event one of the team had inadvertently kicked something with their foot. Again, the conclusion was that it was not the same sound.

We searched for fifteen minutes and still couldn't find the source of the noise, so we decided to head down to the first floor, take a break, and check the video camera to see if the event was captured on video.

Once downstairs, Sarah handed the camera to me, and I rewound the video to a point just prior to the team hearing the sound. In the video, you can see that Sarah is walking slow, in order to minimize camera shake, so I was fairly confident we would have a decent video of the incident, and we did.

The video shows Trigger standing next to Bondsy, taking temperature readings. She indicated the room temperature was fluctuating between eighty and eighty-one degrees. Bondsy mentions how only minutes before, the temperature was at eighty-nine degrees, so there was a temperature fluctuation of eight degrees. Bondsy then asks Sarah to bring the camera to record a shot of the thermometer's LCD screen, to document the current temperature. As Sarah is recording the temperature reading, a noise is heard at the end of the hallway. Both investigator Chris and Bondsy acknowledge the sound at the same time and say, *"Did you hear that?"* Immediately, Chris heads down the hallway in search of the noise.

Once at the end of the hall, and directing his comment to a possible spirit presence, Chris says, *"Can you knock on the door of the room you are in, or tap on something, so I know which room you are in?"*

Next, Bondsy asks Trigger to go to the end of the hallway with Chris, to check for additional temperature fluctuations. I'm not sure if it was due to fear or not, but she did not go as he requested.

As I watched the video, I was surprised Bondsy didn't join Chris at the end of the hall. When I asked him about this, he told me that there was something about the second floor that he did not like, and when they heard the noise, he couldn't force himself to walk to the end of the hallway.

Next the video shows Chris walk into the last room on the right for a few seconds, then return to the hallway. When he comes out of the room, Bondsy asks Trigger for a second time to go to the end of the hallway where Chris is, and check the temperature reading, which she does. He instructs Sarah to stay where she is. I could tell by the tone of his voice; he was feeling uneasy and wanted someone nearby.

Chris then turns toward the group and takes a step forward. As he does this, there is a faint flash of light at the bottom of the wall, just behind him. He immediately reacts and says, *"Did you guys take a picture?"* To which, Trigger responds, *"No!"* He then asks, *"Did you see a flash behind me?"* *"I did, I thought you took a picture,"* replied Sarah. In an excited voice, Chris responds, *"No, I didn't."*

Suddenly, Chris feels extremely cold and asks the group to join him at the end of the hall. Trigger is the first to join him and using the infrared thermometer, begins checking the temperature. Chris points out to Trigger how the hair is standing up on his arm and is covered in goosebumps. Next, Bondsy asks Trigger what the temperature is, and in a visibly shaken voice she replies, *"It's twenty-two" degrees."* This meant, there was a sixty-seven degree drop in room temperature, from the high temperature recorded only minutes before.

For years, paranormal investigators and folks experiencing haunting activity, have reported, and in many cases, have documented extreme drops in temperature during hauntings and investigations. One of the most prevalent beliefs as to the cause of extreme temperature drops is that in order to manifest, ghosts need energy. So, they utilize the heat in the environment of the location they are haunting.

But after investigating the paranormal for more than two decades, I personally believe the extreme temperature drops, are caused either by portals or interdimensional windows opening, when the ghostly entities enter our realm, allowing us to feel the actual temperature from the realm they enter the portal through. Or possibly ghosts, beings, creatures or whatever these mysterious entities are, are void of heat and are so cold, they momentarily affect the natural temperature of our world.

In the video, after hearing the temperature reading, Sarah starts walking slowly down the hall toward Chris. Bondsy who was behind Sarah, and is standing still, tells her not to go too far. When she asks him why, he responds, *"Because I'm getting creeped out!"*

The Granite City investigation was only Bondsy's second paranormal investigation with me. He has been on several investigations since Granite City, and has never reacted in such an uneasy manner, as he did on the second floor of the old YMCA.

After Bondsy replied he was getting, *"Creeped out,"* Sarah retorts, *"If something shuts a door, I want to record it,"* and continues walking slowly toward the end of the hall.

From the video footage, it appears she takes two steps, because with each step she takes, the video moves up and down a bit. After the second step, you can hear the sound of something bouncing on the concrete floor. It sounded like someone threw a coin down the hallway, that skimmed or bounced three times.

When the object bounces, Chris asks, *"Did you do that?,"* referring to Sarah. Bondsy responds first, by saying, *"Sarah, you kicked something,"* to which she replies, *"No I didn't!"*

A priceless piece of video footage occurs just after Sarah declares she didn't kick anything. Because you immediately see Trigger do a quick about face and walk toward Sarah at a fast pace. She has a half grin, half look of terror, on her face that seems to be saying, *"I'm out of here!"*

Bondsy again announces he is feeling, *"Creeped out,"* and by the agitated tone of his voice, you can tell he is serious. Chris shines the light from his flashlight on the floor, searching for the object. He finds an empty .22 caliber shell casing on the floor and tosses it down the hallway, trying to duplicate the sound, but it sounds nothing like the original bouncing object.

After reviewing the video, we decide to take a break, so while Sarah, Trigger, Lil Beans and Chris, head down the street to a local convenience store to pick up, water and soft drinks for everyone, Bondsy and I stay behind to monitor the equipment.

When they left, I decided to head back to the second floor, to see if I could figure out what caused the sound of an object being thrown. Bondsy who was still uneasy, said, *"I'm not going back up there!"*

Having been to many haunted locations over the years and experiencing some pretty unusual and at times frightening things myself. I explained to him how some places, gave me an uneasy feeling as well. But overcoming these feelings is all part of pursuing the unexplained. Knowing he had a strong interest in the paranormal, I further explained that if he didn't go back to the second floor with me, he would regret not facing his fears and it could hinder his pursuit of the paranormal. I told him by going back to the second floor, and facing his fears, his apprehension would go away. After my paranormal pep talk of sorts, he changed his mind and accompanied me to the second floor.

We walked up and down the hallway, searching for evidence of the object that was thrown at them. We tossed, bounced, threw, and kicked everything we found, including a screw, a small rock, chunks of plaster and a nail. None of them sounded like what is heard on the video. Nothing that is, until I found a piece of glass approximately two and a half inches long and a half-inch wide.

When I saw the glass, I kicked it and it sounded similar, but not exactly like the sound in the video. Then I picked it up and tossed it a few feet in front of me. When I did, it bounced several times and sounded identical to what is heard in the video. As soon as Bondsy heard the sound, he immediately said, *"That's it, that's what we heard!"*

To rule out any other possibilities, I dropped the glass to see if maybe it had been lodged in the ceiling and had dropped to the floor. Although it sounded similar, it was not identical, like the sound made after I tossed the chunk of glass. Based on the sound, it appeared the noise was made by a piece of thrown glass. Now the million-dollar question was, who, or what, threw it?

A short time later, the team returned with the refreshments, so we joined the group and explain what we had discovered. During the break, I headed back to the second floor and set up an infrared video camera on a tripod. After setting the camera up, I was headed back to the first floor and was halfway down the stairs, when I heard someone whisper my name, *"Larry!"*

The team was standing at the bottom of the stairs, so I asked if anyone had whispered my name, to which they replied, *"no!"* Unfortunately, no audio recorders were in the immediate area, so there was no recorded evidence of what I heard.

After our break, we headed to the locker-room and pool area to continue the investigation. We walked around for several minutes, exploring the various rooms, before ending up at the swimming pool. Chris and I were standing next to the pool, while the rest of the group was in front of us and to our right.

We were discussing splitting up into three groups of two, when we heard a mysterious shushing sound. It sounded like a person shushing us to be quiet. The sound came from either the doorway behind us or from the room just beyond the doorway.

In unison, Chris and I asked if anyone else heard the shushing sound. As it turned out, we were the only two who heard it, but, within the hour, other members of the team would hear it as well.

Each time we heard it; members of the team were talking. So, the sound was not made by anyone in the group. When I reviewed the audio recorders from the swimming pool area a few days later, I found that we recorded the strange noise on two occasions. So, not only did we physically hear the shushing, we documented it as well.

After hearing the strange shushing, we split up to investigate the pool and locker room area. Bondsy, Trigger, Lil Beans and Chris headed into the shadows for their investigation, while Sarah and I remained in the pool area.

I wanted to do an EVP session and try to communicate with the little girl that we were told had drowned in the swimming pool.

Sarah and I both had tape recorders, so we stood at opposite sides of the pool approximately fifteen feet from one another. Sarah was carrying her recorder and I placed mine at the edge of the pool in front of me.

I began the session by asking routine type questions I usually ask, when conducting an EVP session, such as, *"Who is here, Can you tell me your name* or *How old are you?"* After asking a question, I wait twenty seconds or so, in order to give any entities, present a chance to respond, and allow the recorders to record the response.

Sarah, Bondsy, and the Author by the Pool

After several minutes of asking questions, and not hearing anything, I said to Sarah, *"If a little girl drowned in the pool, and her spirit is present, maybe she would rather talk to another girl. Why don't you ask some questions?"*

So, Sarah, began asking questions. The first question she asked, was, *"Hey little girl, do you like to play with Barbie's?"* Immediately after asking the question, she said in a startled voice, *"I just felt something touch my leg!"* To which I responded, *"No kidding,"* then ask, *"Do you like Sarah?"*

A few days later, while reviewing the audio from the recorder I placed near the edge of the swimming pool, I found I had recorded a whisper that sounds like it says, *"No."* It was recorded immediately after Sarah asked her question. When Sarah reviewed audio from her recorder, she found that she also recorded a voice after asking the question. The voice sounds like a child and is a voice rather than a whisper, and sounds like it is saying, *"Mouse!"*

A few days after the investigation, I brought the EVP I recorded to the radio station, for Bondsy and Sarah to listen to. Bondsy played Sarah's recording first, then mine, so we could compare the two. After playing the clips, Bondsy had an idea. He created two audio tracks, using audio editing software. On one track he imported Sarah's clip and on the other, my recording. He matched up the clips, so they would play at the same time. When playing the voice and the whisper clips together, they clearly say, *"No!"* So, the question is, was the voice the spirit of the little girl who drown in the pool, or that of another phantom child who roams the building?

After investigating the pool, Sarah and I headed back to the second floor where the glass was thrown, while Bondsy, and the rest of the team remained in the locker room area. They didn't have a flashlight with them because they forgot their light in the pool area.

The locker room is like a maze, with several rooms, doorways, twist and turns. It is easy to get turned around in and lost, especially in the dark. Chris had his digital camera with him, so in order to find their way back to the pool area, Bondsy asked him to take a series of flash photos so they could see and find their way back to the pool to get their flashlight.

Immediately after Bondsy asked Chris to take the photos, a loud bang was heard. It sounded like someone threw something that hit and bounced off one of the nearby metal lockers, then hits the floor. Bondsy was recording audio at the time, so the following is the transcript of what was said, minus the swear words which I edited out.

Transcript of the first locker-room bang.

Bondsy: *"Can you take a flash burst with that camera?"*
Chris: *"Yeah."*
Bondsy: *"Then take a whole bunch, dude!"*

Two seconds later, the loud bang occurs, followed by what sounds like the same sound made by the piece of glass, from earlier in the night on the second floor. Immediately after the bang the following exchange is recorded:

Bondsy: *"That is not funny!"*
Chris: *"That's not you Trigger?*
Trigger: *"No, I'm shaking!"*

When Trigger speaks, you can clearly hear fear in the tone of her voice. Unfortunately, this would not be the last incident for Trigger, because a short time later, something eerily similar to what just happened would occur again in the locker room.

Lil Beans and Chris ventured off to check out the pool area, while Bondsy and Trigger remained in the locker room. There is an old sauna, near the locker room. Bill told us earlier about a man who allegedly passed away in the sauna. Bondsy and Trigger decided to take turns sitting inside the sauna to see what they might experience. At one point, while Bondsy is in the Sauna, he heard the door handle to the room jiggle. So, he asks Trigger if she is playing with the handle, to which she responded, *"No!"*

With that, Bondsy becomes uncomfortable being inside the sauna and exits the room. They continued to investigate the locker room, and eventually found themselves passing by the sauna again. As they passed by, Bondsy asks Trigger if she wants to try sitting in the sauna. She starts to answer him, when once again, something bounces off a nearby locker and lands on the floor. Whatever hit the locker, sounded like a nail or piece of glass hitting metal, then bouncing off. The following is a transcript from Bondsy's audio recorder of what transpired.

Bondsy: *"Do you want to go in the sauna?"*
Trigger: *"I guess."*

As soon as Trigger says, *"I guess,"* the loud bang occurs. It sounds similar to the bang that occurred a few minutes earlier. The sound is followed by an expletive from Bondsy and a very nervous giggle from the pair.

Bondsy: *"That's the same damn thing!"*
Trigger: *Laughs nervously.*
Bondsy: *"I want to go back to the pool, is that the way back to the pool?"*
Trigger: *"Oh my God, I don't know!"*
Trigger: *"Here, this is the way back to the pool!"*

With that they leave the area.

Throughout the night, things seemed to happen around Bondsy. I wondered if it had anything to do with the uneasy feeling he developed, while on the second floor. Objects were thrown at, or near members of the group, three times during the night. Only two investigators, Bondsy and Trigger, were present each time it happened. I'm not sure if they were the target of the activity, or if it was a case of being in the right place at the wrong time. Although, being in the right place at the wrong time on three separate occasions in one night, seems to amount to more than mere coincidence.

Having had enough excitement for one night, Bondsy and Trigger met up with Chris and Lil Beans, then the foursome returned upstairs to join Sarah and me. It was just after 3:30 a.m., so we needed to start packing up our equipment, in order to make it back to Springfield for Bondsy and Sarah's 6:00 a.m. radio show. Even though we had to wrap things up a bit early, the night had been an eventful one, and one we would not soon forget.

In my years investigating the supernatural, I have found that physical interaction with unseen forces is rare. In fact, the only experience more uncommon has been witnessing actual apparitions, which I have seen seven in the two decades I have been investigating. Whether the entities throwing the objects, were spirits, or some other life force that we have not yet identified, remains to be seen.

The interaction at the YMCA was in the form of material objects being thrown. Whether they were thrown at, or simply near the investigative team, is unknown. But something was certainly trying to get our attention. I'm also not sure how the objects were thrown. Was it by a non-physical spirit hand or some other form of supernatural manipulation of the objects. Whatever the case, it happened three times during the night.

It certainly seemed like something wanted us to know that they were there, but why? This is speculation on my part, but I wonder if the thrown objects was simply an attempt to scare us into leaving. I say this because when we tried to communicate by conducting EVP sessions, the only response we received was by the swimming pool, when Sarah asked questions of the little girl. Not only did Sarah get a response, but she immediately reacted to a physical sensation of something touching her leg.

The majority of the interactions were unprovoked. The shushing sound, that we heard and recorded while in the pool area, also seemed to be an unprovoked interaction as well. Unless our voices were disturbing the ghost and was all the provocation they needed. The shushing was reminiscent of the stern reprimands administered by teachers and librarians to noisy students.

The old YMCA is a large building and we experienced activity throughout the facility. Does this mean that several spirits roam the location and were interacting with us? Or did a particular phantom tag along and follow us around the building? My gut feeling is there is more than one ghostly entity in the building.

The common denominators in relationship to the objects being thrown, seemed to be Bondsy and Trigger. As both were present every time it happened. Were they merely in the right place at the wrong time when the objects were thrown, three separate times? Author Ian Fleming once said: *"Once is Happenstance, twice is Coincidence, and Three Times is*

Enemy Action."

Bondsy was clearly uncomfortable during the investigation, especially while on the second floor. Was something intentionally trying to unnerve him, or was that sixth sense we all have, trying to warn him and keep him out of harm's way ?

I agree with Bondsy, there is something unusual about the second floor near the stairwell. It definitely gives off an eerie feeling at times.

The drastic temperature change was recorded on the second floor as well, when the temperature dropped from eighty-degrees to twenty-two degrees in an instant.

Did our personal experiences during the night of July 25th, 2013, offer proof that something paranormal is going on in the old Granite City YMCA building? Well, if hearing and recording disembodied voices, having objects thrown through the air by invisible forces, and experiencing a sixty-degree temperature drop in a matter of seconds qualifies as paranormal, then I guess it is safe to say, *"Yes, I believe they do, and I also believe the building is haunted."*

If you are fortunate enough to get the chance to investigate the old YMCA in Granite City Illinois, you may want to take a safety helmet along, just in case the spirits roaming the halls of the old building, decide to throw a few objects your way.

Iowa

FARRAR SCHOOL

FIVE

No more pencils and no more books,
No more teachers' dirty looks
Schools Out for summer
Schools Out till fall
We might not come back at all

The above lyrics, from Alice Cooper's 1972 hit, Schools Out, may not apply to the children who once attended the Farrar School in Farrar, Iowa. As many, including myself, believe they never actually left.

Eyewitness accounts of ghost children seen standing on the stairs, and doors to hallway lockers slamming shut on their own, have led many to believe that class is still in session at this one-time bustling area school. When I say, class is in session, I mean it is in session twenty-four hours a day.

During our investigation, I tried my hand as a substitute math teacher and amazingly, someone or something responded to my impromptu math quiz. Making it more interesting is the fact that not only did something respond, but they responded with the correct answers. Even more remarkable is the fact that not only did we hear the responses, we recorded them as well. You will read about this shortly.

Over the years some claim to have witnessed a tall Shadow Man, standing seven feet tall, at various locations in the building. Sound farfetched? Well, I thought so too, until I saw him for myself during our October 2013 investigation.

Schools are safe welcoming places for the most part, but there is an eeriness about them when the building sets empty. The feeling or vibration it gives off changes once the children are gone. Much like one of R.L. Stine's, Goosebumps books, our imagination turns the environment from a warm and loving learning place to a location that nightmares are made of.

A brief history of Farrar

Farrar is an unincorporated community located in Polk County, Iowa, consisting of a few homes, a church, cemetery and the 17,000 square foot school building. The area's population has been on the decline for many years, like much of rural America has.

According to the Farrar School website, in 1919, local farmer, C.G. Geddes donated the property where the school sits today. When it was built, the plan was to have all of the areas one room country schoolhouses merge into one local area school that would be known as the Washington Township Consolidated School District.

Farrar School was built, and a dedication ceremony took place on April 1st, 1922. Locals gathered for the celebration and dedication of the new school. But it seems not all citizens were behind the new building, with its $100,000 price tag. Some refused to attend the celebration calling it, *"A monument to the arrogance and vanity of the school board!"* To some, it seemed that a boiler heating system, electric lights, and indoor bathroom facilities was overkill for a school.

On May 3rd, 2002, the eighty-year-old schoolhouse closed and remained unused until current owners Jim and Nancy Oliver purchased the building in December of 2006.

The Oliver's who are in the process of restoring the building, live in a portion of the school, which serves as their home. Soon after they moved into the building, they began noticing things that led them to believe they were not alone. Nancy Oliver described several incidents during our walkthrough of the building prior to our investigation.

One incident took place on a staircase when she lost her balance and almost fell. She said she felt a hand on her shoulder, that helped her regain her balance, and prevented her from falling. Thinking it was her husband who had helped her, she turned to thank him, but found that no one was there.

A dark distinct outline of a small boy has been seen on the stairway that goes down to the gymnasium. The boy was described as being three and a half feet tall, standing on the stairs and holding onto the handrail. The figure was motionless for several seconds before disappearing.

Over the years, students and employees of the school have reported strange and unexplained activity. Experiences that range from hearing disembodied voices, unexplained noises and seeing apparitions. Psychics visiting the location claim that spirits of the dead occupy the former school. Others, including paranormal investigators, have witnessed unusual activity.

I first heard of the Farrar School in 2011, on one of the many television shows about ghost and hauntings. The idea of investigating a former school seemed inviting to me, as I had investigated many different types of buildings, but never an old school.

When I decided to investigate Farrar, I knew my friends, Bondsy and Sarah from the radio station, were looking for a location to investigate for their 2013 Halloween show, and the school seemed like the perfect place. As you continue reading this book, you will notice a reoccurring theme of Bondsy and his radio crew joining me on investigations. This location would be no different, because when I brought up the prospect of investigating a large creepy building, reportedly haunted by the ghost of children, Bondsy was all for it.

Accompanying me on the Farrar trip would be Bondsy and Sarah, along with investigator Chris, who accompanied us on the Granite City, Illinois YMCA investigation.

The longer I am involved investigating the supernatural, the more I notice odd things taking place prior to investigations, that some would call coincidence while others like me, call synchronistic or unusual. The occurrences although nothing too exciting or earth shattering, are things that cause me to take note and scratch my head and say, *"What the heck."*

On the day of the Farrar investigation, a couple of strange incidents occurred. The first took place when I stopped at a local gas station to put fuel in my SUV, before picking up the team for the investigation. The occurrence once again involved the 11:11 phenomena I mentioned in the chapter on the Granite City investigation.

When I finished putting fuel in my vehicle and the pump clicked off, I noticed the total gallons came to 11.11 gallons of gas. Because of my experience with the 11:11 phenomena, seeing the number staring back at me, immediately gained my attention. Again, it was nothing earth shattering, but nonetheless, seemed par for the course on a day I would be investigating a haunted school. It gave me the feeling that something out there, wanted me to know it knew I was delving into the supernatural again.

After the incident, I picked up the team and we headed to Iowa. We had been on the road for about three hours, when Sarah realized she forgot to bring the charger for her cell phone. So, we pulled off the highway and stopped at a large truck stop, to see if they had a charger that was compatible with her phone. This is when the second of the two unusual occurrences happened.

We pulled into a parking space, near the front entrance of the store. Bondsy and Chris exited the vehicle first and went inside. I waited for Sarah to exit the vehicle, so I could lock the doors, then we followed behind the other two. When I entered the store, I saw Chris browsing in one of the aisles. Bondsy was heading toward the soda fountain area, but I lost track of him because I couldn't see him from where I was standing. Sarah was nearby looking for a phone charger. I noticed a man walk out of the men's bathroom and saw the door close behind him. I needed to use the bathroom before we hit the road again, so I headed that way.

The door to the bathroom was the type that didn't have a doorknob on the outside, but simply had a shiny metal plate where the handle would be. Walking toward the door at a steady pace and with both of my arms extended; I pushed the door with the palms of my hands. Both of my hands hit the door at the same time. I was totally surprised when my body sort of bounced backward, as the door didn't budge. It didn't budge because it was locked. I pushed against it a second time, with a fair amount of force, but it still wouldn't open.

This seemed odd because I hadn't seen anyone enter the bathroom after the man came out. I looked around the store and only saw Sarah and Chris, so I figured that Bondsy must have slipped into the bathroom without me noticing him and locked the door. I waited outside the door, looking at some nearby merchandise, when I saw Chris coming toward me. He passed directly by, and in the same manner as I had done, pushed the bathroom door with both hands. This time, however, it opened.

When I saw the door open, my mouth dropped, because I couldn't believe what I saw. Only seconds before, the door was locked. I turned my head to the left as something caught my attention. It was Bondsy still by the soda fountain on the other side of the store. So, he hadn't been in the bathroom.

Walking over to the bathroom door I pushed it with one arm, and it opened. I walked inside and looked around. No one was in the room, but Chris. I asked him if Bondsy was in the bathroom before he entered and he said the bathroom was empty when he walked in.

I explained what happened, when I tried to enter through the door and how it was locked. He reassured me, that no one was in the bathroom before he entered, and the door was unlocked. While in the bathroom, I checked and there is only one way in and out of the room. Examining the bathroom door, I found that just as I thought, there is no lock on it. So, the door could not have been locked.

Perplexed by what happened, I mentioned it to Bondsy, as we were leaving the store, and he assured me that he had not been in the bathroom either. So, I don't know what happened, but there wasn't a logical explanation for the door not opening when I pushed on it.

Farrar is located twenty-five miles northeast of Des Moines in a rural area. After turning off of Interstate 80, we headed down several narrow country roads, arriving at the school around 8:00 p.m. Lightening was flashing off in the distance, making for a perfect setting for a paranormal adventure.

Soon after arriving, we were joined by owner Nancy Oliver, who gave us a tour of the building. She told us about the time she witnessed a small boy on the well-lit stairwell that leads down to the gymnasium. The boy appeared to be between three and four feet tall. He was standing motionless with one foot on each step, holding onto the handrail. After a couple of seconds, he vanished into thin air.

I asked her if anything tragic had happened at the school that may have led to the haunting. She explained there are rumors that a janitor was suspected of molesting children at the school. As the story goes, the principal at the time was aware of what was happening and may have covered up what the janitor had done.

Nancy knew the name of the janitor, but would not divulge

the information, because his family still lives in the area.

Another intriguing yet hard to believe story Nancy told us, would turn into reality for me early on in our investigation. Because in a few short hours, I would witness exactly what she was about to describe.

Nancy began her story by telling about a group of paranormal enthusiast who investigated the school a few years before us. One member of the group was a talented artist and during their investigation, witnessed a type of paranormal entity, I had heard reports of, but up until this night had never witnessed for myself.

Nancy explained that the man witnessed an incredible sight and told her, if he hadn't seen it with his own eyes, would not have believed it. What he saw has also been reported by other witnesses investigating the building.

The man claimed he saw a solid, dark, silhouette of a person walking through the building. He knew it wasn't a member of his team because of the incredible size of the phantom he witnessed. He described it as being at least seven feet tall and extremely thin, moving its arms and legs back and forth as it walked through the building.

Being an artist, the man drew a sketch of what he saw and gave it to Nancy. She showed the drawing to us and, I must admit, even though I am as open minded as the next person, I found the enormous size of what he described, hard to believe. He claimed what he saw was not simply a cast shadow, but the shadow was a being of some type. What he described is known by paranormal investigators, as a *shadow person*.

What stood out most about the sketch of the *shadow person* was the great detail the man put into the drawing. It was as though it had not only been etched on the drawing paper but etched in the memory of the witness forever. After showing us the drawing of the *shadow person*, Nancy took us to the gym, which is actually a level below the first floor of the building. When entering the gymnasium, to the right, are three rooms. The girl's bathroom, a boy's bathroom, and the former coach's office. To the left, and in the corner, was a doorway. Nancy explained the doorway led to the boiler room and after passing through the boiler room, is the fuel room, where fuel for the furnace was stored. The boiler room was also used by the janitors as a workshop and was a place they spent a great deal of time when school was in session.

Also, on the left and against the wall, were a set of bleachers, several rows high. We stood on the bleachers and had Nancy take several photos of us as a group. While doing this, I noticed fastened to the wall, just behind the bleachers, was what remained of some type of a metal bracket. It was three feet wide and approximately five to six feet high. The bottom of the bracket was six feet off the floor. I know this because, later in the evening, I had Bondsy, who is 6'-1", stand under the bracket. The top of his head was barely above the bottom of the bracket. You will see the importance of this observation, shortly.

When Nancy finished her walkthrough, we retrieved our equipment from my vehicle, and Nancy returned to the first-floor area that she and husband Jim, converted into their living quarters.

We strategically placed Sony audio recorders throughout the building and began setting up our infrared surveillance cameras. Based on what I would soon witness, I have since changed the procedures used when setting up the video surveillance system. At the time, the procedure I used, was to place all cameras strategically throughout the location, then once all cameras were in place, and camera angles set, I would start the recording for all cameras at the same time. I did this so that the time stamp for all cameras, was the same.

We used the second-floor hallway as the staging area for the surveillance system. I set up a table and placed the video monitor and DVR on it. Three infrared cameras were already in place and connected to the DVR. One camera on the first floor, pointed at a section of lockers with their doors wide open. I placed the camera in this manner in hopes of recording the doors slamming shut, which had been reported by others investigating the building. A second camera was pointed at the principal's office and a third was placed in the center of the gymnasium, pointed at the bleachers along the wall on the left side of the gym.

At the time, Bondsy was on the first floor and Chris was in the men's bathroom in the gym area. Sarah was standing a few feet from me while I finished hooking up the fourth and final video camera to the DVR. The camera I was hooking up was the camera placed on the third floor, monitoring the hallway.

As I was hooking up camera four, I looked at the video monitor and could see the video feeds from cameras one, two and three were working fine. Suddenly, something from the feed of camera three, which had been placed in the gymnasium, caught my eye. It caused me to do a double take, because it looked like something dark was moving across the gym floor.

Immediately I stopped what I was doing to take a closer look at the monitor. I couldn't believe what I saw. Because, walking across the center of the gym floor, directly in front of the bleachers, was a tall, black, shadowy figure. It was no ordinary shadow; it was the shadow of a person. Due to the height of the being, I immediately knew I was watching the shadow man that Nancy described to us during the walkthrough. It was swinging its arms and legs as it walked in front of the bleachers, headed toward the door leading to the janitor's room. What I saw, was not a shadow cast by an entity, the shadow, was the entity! It appeared to be intelligent due to the way it was walking, like it was on a mission to get to the other side of the gym.

The video camera, which is equipped with infrared, was located thirty feet from the bottom row of the bleachers and was sitting on a six-inch-high tripod placed on the gym floor. The range of the camera I was using is sixty-five feet. If you have ever seen video filmed in infrared, you know the clearest and brightest portion of the video, is the center. The outer or peripheral edges of the scene appear darker as images get out of range of the infrared lighting.

So even though I could see the corner of the gym where the door leading to the janitor's room is located, it was much darker in the corner than the center of the gym. I point this out, because I want to emphasize just how dark and dense the shadow person I was watching on the monitor was. The figure was so dark, I could still see it as it walked in the dark shadows at the far side of the gym. So, the figure was, darker than the dark obscure corner of the gym.

It took several seconds to rationalize what I was seeing and determine I was not witnessing the shadow or reflection of one of the team members who may have wandered in the gym without me knowing it. By the time I was certain I was seeing the shadow person Nancy told us about, the figure was almost to the corner of the gym. It was at this point, I excitedly yelled out, *"There's a shadow man walking across the gym!"* Sarah, not knowing what I was talking about, hurried over to take a look. By the time she made it over to the monitor, the shadowy figure had already disappeared into the darkness.

I ran down the stairs, headed for the gym, yelling out to Bondsy and Chris, *"Where are you guys?"* I wanted to know their location, to make sure neither were in the gym. Bondsy yelled back, that he was on the first floor. Chris, didn't respond, but I soon found out he was in the boy's bathroom in the gym at the time, so neither of them could have cast the shadow.

As exciting as witnessing the shadow man was, it was also one of my most disappointing moments as a paranormal investigator. I say this, because while I was setting up the surveillance system and directionally adjusting camera angles, I was not yet recording video. So, I may have missed out on the video shot of a lifetime. Because if I could see the shadow figure on the monitor, I should have recorded it as well.

What I saw was similar to the artist drawing with a couple of distinctions. The artist described what he saw, as very thin and extremely tall, estimating the shadowy being was seven feet tall. This may sound far-fetched, but I say with confidence, that what I saw, was at minimum, seven feet tall as well. The reason for my confidence is due to the old metal bracket on the wall I mentioned earlier.

Made from angle iron, the bracket was five feet in height, three feet wide and rectangular in shape. I assume it is a remnant of some type of gym equipment that once hung from the wall. When the shadow figure walked across the room from right to left, it passed in front of the bracket. The top of the head of the creature was approximately eighteen inches above the bottom edge of the bracket. Later, when I used Bondsy as a human measuring stick, I had him stand under the bracket to see where the top of his head was in comparison to the bottom of the bracket. As it turned out, the top of Bondsy's head was only an inch above the bottom of the bracket. So, the shadow man I saw was at least eighteen inches taller than Bondsy, meaning the figure stood seven to seven and a half feet tall!

The figure the artist drew was thin in comparison to what I saw. Plus, it looked like it was wearing a long black coat and a short-rimmed cap, like an old sea captain would wear. The main difference, however, is the figure appeared to have a large protruding stomach or potbelly. So, does this mean there is more than one of the shadow people roaming Farrar School, or do they change in appearance over time like we do by gaining or losing mass?

In November of 2014, I saw a television show called *Ghost Stalkers*. The show is about a two-man team of paranormal investigators and the episode I saw was about their investigation of Farrar school. I bring up the show, because one of the investigators claimed he witnessed the shadow man in an upstairs hallway. What caught my attention was his description of what he saw, because he indicated it had some type of protrusion or abnormality around the midsection. The investigator described seeing the shadow person as it moved toward him. I saw it from the side or more of a profile view. Was the protrusion, the potbelly I witnessed, only from a different angle?

After the excitement of witnessing the shadow man died down, we finished setting up the equipment and began our investigation. But it wouldn't take long, before we had our second bit of excitement for the night. It occured while Sarah and I were on the third floor in one of the old classrooms. Chris and Bondsy were on the second floor investigating together, or so we thought. We didn't know that Chris had told Bondsy he was going down to the gym. He was under the

Second Floor Hallway-Farrar School

impression Bondsy was following him and would be right behind him as he headed to the gym. When he got to the bottom of the steps he started to walk toward the gym. After taking a step or two, he heard something behind him that caused him to stop dead in his tracks. He later told us he heard what sounded like a large person exhaling. Even though Sarah and I were on the third floor, we heard Chris call out. He first yelled, *"Bondsy,"* paused momentarily, then called out Bondsy's name again. Next, he called out my name, *"Larry,"* two times as well.

Hearing Chris, Bondsy shouted, *"What do you want?"* There was no response, so he headed downstairs to look for him. He met Chris coming up the stairs, as Chris decided, rather than hang around by himself in the dark with a heavy breathing phantom that exhaled like Michael Myers from the Halloween slasher films, he would head back up the stairs, where there would be safety in numbers. In doing so, he would have to pass by whatever made the breathy sound.

By this time, Sarah and I were enroute downstairs to see what all the excitement was about. When we got to the first floor, Chris, was having a discussion with Bondsy. He seemed both perturbed and shook up. Perturbed, because he was under the impression Bondsy was going to follow him downstairs and shook up because of what he heard.

He explained that after hearing the exhale, he stopped dead in his tracks. He slowly turned around not knowing what he might see. When he did, no one was there. *"A cold chill went down my spine and the hair stood up on the back of my neck,"* he said. *"I knew what I heard and knew no one was down there but me, so I was alone in the dark with who or whatever exhaled, and it was loud!"*

Even though he didn't see anyone, Chris knew that he heard a loud human sounding breath, which meant if it was still there, it was between him and the stairs that led back up to where Bondsy was. So, at first, rather than chance going by whatever might be there, he called out for Bondsy and me. When no one replied, he had no choice but to go back the way he came and pass by the area where the breathy sound came from.

I knew Chris encountered something at the bottom of the staircase, because he was legitimately shook up. But it's hard to grasp the magnitude of a situation, based on someone else's experience. However, nothing beats a personal experience that can be validated by documented evidence, which is exactly what happened in this case.

Earlier in the evening, I placed a digital audio recorder on a table at the far side of the gym near the girls bathroom. The recorder was at least, one hundred feet from where Chris had his encounter with the breath. Several days after the Farrar investigation, I was reviewing audio from the aforementioned recorder. Farrar was one of the first locations I used Sony recorders, to replace my older RCA devices. I found the quality and clarity of recordings were much better using the new recorders. Even at a distance of one hundred feet, the clarity was incredible.

When I played back the audio sequence from Chris's encounter, I could clearly hear his footsteps as he was coming down the stairs. Then I heard a loud and clear, what I can best describe as a sigh or exhale. As soon as I heard the breathy exhale, Chris stop dead in his tracks. Just listening to it sent a cold chill down my spine. I can only imagine how unnerving it would be to hear a breath behind you, in a dark hallway, in a building like the Farrar School. The recorder confirmed everything Chris said he experienced and happened exactly the way he described it.

A third, and truly unique, paranormal experience took place a short time later in a third-floor classroom. The experience confirmed for me that whatever haunts the Farrar School, has intelligence, and does not simply wander aimlessly down the hallways of this once bustling school.

The experience took place shortly after Chris and Bondsy investigated a classroom where they were startled by a loud banging sound, that came out of the blue.

When the banging occurred, Sarah and I were down the hall investigating. We didn't hear it, but we heard the two investigators yell out, as if something was going on. A short time after their excitement, the pair re-joined us to explain what had happened.

They were in an old classroom at the end of the third-floor hallway, listening for the source of a noise they had been hearing. One of the investigators made a comment to the other about how quiet it was in the room. As soon as this was said, a loud metallic banging occurred, which startled both investigators. Trying to figure out what cause the bang, they discovered a folded cafeteria style table leaning against the back wall in the room. What they heard was similar to the sound of someone taking hold of un-folded metal table legs and slamming them closed.

Bondsy recorded the sound, and played it for Sarah and me, so we could hear what they heard. After listening to the recording, Bondsy and I decided to return to the classroom to see if anything else would happen, while Sarah and Chris continued investigating rooms at the opposite end of the hallway.

The room was quiet when we walked in. Bondsy showed me where he and Chris were standing when the banging occurred. While we were discussing their experience, I had an idea. Since this was a former school, and all the desks were still in the classroom, why not conduct math class. Because if the spirits of children who attended the school were still around, what better way to draw a reaction from them, then by holding class. Bondsy sat on the floor at the back of the room and leaned against the wall. I walked to the front of the room and stood like a teacher would if they were conducting class. In an authoritative voice I said, *"My name is Mr. Wilson, I will be your substitute teacher for the day. Please take your seats as it is time to start math class.*

Math Classroom

My plan was to ask simple addition and subtraction questions. So, I announced out loud, that when I asked a question, in order to answer it, anyone present should knock on something loud enough for us to hear. Little did I know that what we were about to experience, would be one of the most incredible encounters I would ever witness.

The first question I asked was, *"What is one plus one?"* It was only a few seconds when we heard a clear, *Knock-Knock,"* which was the correct answer to the question I asked. After hearing the knocks, I said, *"Did you hear that?"*

"I did," Bondsy replied. *"Where did it come from?"*
It came from the floor," I answered.

It sounded like someone, or something knocked on the floor with his or her knuckles and came from between where Bondsy was sitting, and I was standing.

The response to the second question was no less amazing.

I asked, *"What is one plus zero?"* Immediately we heard a *single knock* that also came from the floor. I was so surprised by how quick the response was that I asked Bondsy, *"Was that you?"* Not answering my question, he replied by saying, *"Did you hear that?*

"Yeah," I answered.
"That's not you?"
"No," I replied.
"You're not moving your feet or anything?"
"No, I'm standing perfectly still!"

Next, I said to the phantom student or students, *"The first answers were right, can you answer again by knocking?"* Then asked, *"What's one, plus one?"* Immediately and louder than before, we heard and recorded, *"Knock-Knock!"*

In an excited voice, Bondsy said, *"Dude, did you freaking hear that?"*

"I did," I replied.
"Holy Shit!" He exclaimed.

The mock classroom experiment went on for thirty minutes. During the experiment, I asked twenty questions, and we recorded nine clear, accurate, responses. We actually heard more responses than we recorded, but several were apparently too faint for the recorder to pick up.

Even after hearing clear and accurate responses, what we were hearing, seemed too good to be true. So much so, we continually questioned one another as to whether they had inadvertently caused the knocking sound. At some point who, or whatever was causing the knocking, decided to prove to us that, *"Hey guys, it's not you, it's me,* because, when I asked the next question, I said, *"Last question. What is one, plus one, plus one?"* This time instead of hearing knocking sounds, the response was, *"Click, Click, Click!"* It sounded like someone flicking their tongue against the roof of their mouth, making a *clicking* sound, and a bit like someone hitting two wooden blocks together.

Immediately Bondsy responded with a colorful four-letter word, so, in order to keep this a *G-rated* book, I will simply alter, what he said.

His response to me was, *"Did you Freaking hear that?"*
To which I asked, *"Is that you?"*
"No!"

During the EVP session, I asked a question related to the gender of who, or what, was responding to us, by saying, *"Let's try this for extra-extra credit. I just need to know if you are a boy or a girl. If you are a boy, knock once, for a girl, knock twice!"* No sooner then I said the word, *"twice,"* there was an immediate, loud, single, knock. Indicating it was a boy who was responding to my questions.

I also asked a question related to the grade in school our invisible friend was in. In our audio recording, you hear me say, *"Can you knock and tell us what grade you're in? Just make as many knocks on the floor as the grade you are in! One for first, two for the second."* I started to say three for the third grade, but my questioning was cut off because as soon as I said, *"Two for the second grade,"* there were three distinct knocks in rapid succession, signifying he was in the third grade.

"Did you hear that?" Bondsy asked.
"Three, third," meaning third grade, I responded.
"Yup!"

What Bondsy and I experienced during the mock class experiment, was the most validating interaction I have experienced in all the years that I have been investigating the paranormal. There is no doubt in my mind, that something intelligent was with us in that classroom on October 4th, 2013. Based on the responses we received, we were communicating with a third-grade boy. The average age for a third-grade student is eight or nine years old. I wondered if we were communicating with the little boy seen by Nancy on the stairway. She described him as being approximately three and a half feet tall, which would be close to the height for an eight or nine-year-old child.

The way the questions were answered made sense to me. Responses for the addition questions were a bit slower, like they were trying to figure out the answer, which would be something that a third grader might do. But questions related to gender and grade in school, which they would readily know, were answered without hesitation.

After our classroom experiment, we met up with Sarah and Chris and headed to the first-floor area the Oliver's had set up for investigators to take breaks. We discussed our experience in the classroom and played back some of the responses we recorded. After the break, we returned to the classroom, and tried the math test again. Unfortunately, we didn't get the same results, but did hear the clicking sound again. It sounded like it was coming from somewhere in the middle of our group as we were seated in desks. Interestingly, it didn't start until we discussed moving to another part of the building. Almost as though it was trying to entice us to stay in the room.

During the course of the night, we investigated the old janitor's room, located on the same level as the gym. Of all the places in the building, this was the only location that gave me a creepy, uneasy feeling. But after all, it was located in a damp and dingy part of the building, with an old boiler, workshop area, and a reputation as a place where a janitor, alleged to have molested children, hung out.

We had been in the janitor's area for twenty minutes when we heard tapping sounds that were coming from above us. There was a bit of a breeze outside due to a thunderstorm that was in the area, so I figured the noise was caused by the old ductwork above us, vibrating and rattling. As we were discussing the tapping sound, we heard a loud noise, that originated from the first floor. It sounded as if someone was upstairs moving around. The noise was loud enough to cause us to hurry out of the janitor's area and run upstairs to check it out. When we got to the first floor, the noise stopped, and we found nothing.

The last area of the building we investigated was the third-floor auditorium. We spread out with each of us sitting on a different side of the room. At one point, Sarah sat at a table on the auditorium stage. Speaking aloud, she invited any spirits present to sit with her at the table and make noise, so we would know they were around. Unfortunately, no specters took her up on her offer. We conducted a final EVP session but neither heard nor recorded any responses. It was approaching 4:00 a.m., so we decided to call it a night, and began to break down the equipment and pack up, as we had a five-hour drive ahead of us. But what a night it was.

If someone asked me to recommend a place where they would have a better than average chance to experience paranormal activity. The Farrar School in Iowa would be one of the top ten places I would recommend to them.

After our experiences during the night of October 4th, 2013, I have little doubt that something unusual takes place in the halls and classrooms of this once charming old school. It seems that some of the former students and staff still roam the building, holding on to a time that meant so much to them, refusing to leave. Or did something more sinister in their living years steal their innocence from them? If the children remain, are they trying to reclaim the memories of their childhood that were taken from them? If this is the case, I hope the interaction Bondsy and I had in the classroom, somehow helps to restore what was lost, due to the actions of those they trusted and looked up to.

If children haunt the school, do those who taught them or worked at the school in some capacity, haunt the building as well? If the reports of child abuse, and a cover up are true, do those involved haunt the school in shame? Or were they falsely accused of wrongdoing, themselves victims of misunderstandings that unjustly robbed their reputation and dignity from them? If so, does a piece of them wander the halls of Farrar seeking to clear their name and regain their reputation?

Our entire team personally experienced the strangeness the old school has to offer during the investigation. I must admit, when Nancy showed us the drawing of the shadow man that the witness drew, I was skeptical of the accuracy of what he claimed to see. Little did I know that a short time later, I would see the exact same creature roaming across the gymnasium floor. What I saw was not a shadow cast on the wall, because what I saw walked in front of the bleachers and walked with purpose as if it knew where it was going.

Was the breath that Chris heard, made by the shadow man? It had to be caused by something large, because it was recorded by an audio recorder one-hundred feet from where the sound took place. I believe, who or whatever made the sound, intended to startle the investigator. But was the intent malicious or was it simply having a good laugh at Chris's expense. Either way, the noise was made by something that knew he was there.

The experience Bondsy and I had during the impromptu classroom experiment, was one of the clearest and most validating interactions I have had in my more than two-decades investigating the paranormal and is something neither Bondsy nor I will soon forget. There is no doubt that something intelligent, was with us in the classroom that night. Even more satisfying, we were able to record the interaction on our audio recorder.

Encountering the supernatural is an enlightening and humbling experience. I say this because, it seems when we have a paranormal experience, it is because something not of this world allows us to glimpse a part of reality that, for the most part, we have been told by our peers, doesn't exist.

Many people asked me why I continue investigating the paranormal after so many years. Is it due to curiosity or the thrill of adventure? This may have been the reasons in the beginning, but now that I have seen the strangeness that the paranormal offers, I want to see more of it, and it doesn't get any stranger than what goes on at Farrar School.

MALVERN MANOR

SIX

One advantage of writing books about my adventures investigating the paranormal, has been meeting local radio and television personalities with an interest in the paranormal. In 2011, I was invited to be a guest on the popular Springfield, Illinois morning radio show, *"The Morning Grind,"* hosted by Jason *"Bondsy"* Bond.

Bondsy, who had an interest in the paranormal, although a skeptical one, heard about my first book, *"Chasing Shadows,"* and invited me to be a guest on his Halloween show, to tell a few stories about my experiences as a paranormal investigator. After hearing my stories, his healthy skepticism of the supernatural, led to my invitation for him to tag along with me on an investigation, to see for himself what the paranormal has to offer. Well, as they say, the rest is history. Because, the first place I took him, things happened he couldn't explain.

Each year, since 2011, I take Bondsy and employees from the station, usually interns, on an investigation or two during the summer. Then on Halloween, we discuss the investigations and play unusual audio evidence that was recorded.

On August 9, 2019, I took Bondsy and interns, Lauren, and Kate, to spend the night at one of Iowa's most infamous haunted locations, Malvern Manor. Taking Bondsy and his staff on investigations is rewarding for me, because it gives those not yet convinced the paranormal is real, the opportunity to experience the type of things I have witnessed over the last two decades.

Since 2011, I have taken Bondsy and seven of his staff on nine investigations. Each staff member, without exception, have witnessed things they cannot explain. The 2019 trip would be no exception and would be a night none of us would soon forget.

Malvern Manor was built in the late 1800s as a family-run hotel. It prospered because of its close proximity to the railroad and the many traveling salesmen who spent the night there. Unfortunately, with the advent of the automobile, and the decrease in rail travel, the hotel closed. In the mid-1900s, the manor was the personal residence to the Gibson family.

T.D. Gibson and his wife were not the biological parents of their children, as the children's parents were declared unfit to raise them. So, they were sent to live with the Gibson's who were their aunt and uncle. The separation from her biological parents emotionally affected the youngest child, Inez,

According to stories, one day, Inez told her brother Otto, she was going outside to jump rope. Later that day, when Otto walked into her room, he found his sister with a jump rope around her neck, hanging from inside of the closet. The cause of death was determined to be accidental, but rumors circulated that the true cause was emotional stress because of a drop in her grades. Visitors to the home have reported hearing the voice of a child coming from her room, and some believe it is the spirit of Inez.

After the days of the Gibson family, the building was converted into a combination convalescent home and minimum care facility, housing an array of patients, ranging from alcoholics to schizophrenics. It is alleged that because of the varied array of disorders, the care the patients received was lacking. Some believe that the alleged lack of care has led to the haunting activity taking place at the manor.

During the over six hour, four-hundred-mile trip, Bondsy ask me to tell a few stories of some of the unexplained things that I have witnessed over the years. One story I told was about the strange things that happened to me after I returned home from an investigation at another famous Iowa haunt, the Villisca Ax Murder house, which coincidentally is only thirty-eight miles from Malvern Manor. During the story, I explained how I would hear a strange voice whisper my name in my right ear after returning home from the house. The importance of this story will be apparent soon.

I scheduled us to meet owner Kurt Fricke at 6:00 p.m., but we arrived early. So, we had supper at one of the local eating establishments. While we were waiting for our food. Kate said to Lauren, *"Did you tell Larry what happened to you?" "No, I almost forgot,"* Lauren replied.

Curious about what Kate said, I asked Lauren if something happened to her.

"Yes," she replied. *"It was really weird. Do you remember when you were telling the story about the murder house and mentioned how you would hear your name whispered in your ear,"* she asked.

"Sure, I do," I replied. *"Why?"*

"Well after you told the story, I shut my eyes to take a nap. I know I wasn't asleep when I heard a voice whisper my name in my ear. It was freaky!"

Since this has happened to others. I asked Lauren, *"Which ear did you hear the whisper in?"* To which she replied, *"My right ear."* Which was the ear I would hear my name called.

What Lauren experienced has happened to others when I talk about the murder house. So, I believed her. But hearing the whisper was only the beginning of strange things that Lauren would experience on this night.

When supper was over, it was time to meet the owner, so we headed to the manor. Kurt greeted us with a handshake, and a smile, then began a brief tour of the building. He first took us to an area known as the nurses wing. At the end of the hall leading to the nurses wing, is an old nurses station, with a counter and storage bins where the residents medical charts were kept. At the convergence of the main hall and nurses station is another hallway, known as the shadow man hallway. Named for Malvern Manor's shadowy phantom, often seen in the dark corridors of this area of the building. Some who have experienced the shadow man, have felt a malevolent energy when it is present.

According to Kurt, several female investigators visiting the manor claim that a shadowy figure followed them out of the hallway and into the main part of the manor. I am not sure why, but the nurses wing and the shadow man hallway gave me an eerie feeling. It was a feeling that you are not alone, and someone or something was watching. With this being said, it didn't take long before the weirdness started.

Bondsy, was recording video with his cellphone, while Kurt was describing activity that has been experienced in the hallway. Suddenly, he interrupted Kurt, because he saw an unusual white light move in front of his cellphone, while recording. He replayed the video, and we could see a bright white light come out of nowhere and move in front of his cell phone. The odd thing about the light appearing is the doors to the adjacent rooms were closed. So, the hall was dark with no available source to cause the light. I have reviewed hundreds of hours of video from investigations and am familiar with light anomalies caused by dust, moisture, and pollen particles. With certainty, I can say the light Bondsy recorded was not caused by any of those. It was simply a white light that passed or flashed in front of his cell phone camera. After the brief excitement, we continued down the hallway to room seven.

To get to room seven, you turn right at the nurses station, and it is the last room on the righthand side. Kurt stopped us before entering the room to tell a story about an exquisite woman who was committed to the manor when it was a home for the mentally ill. Some believe that her spirit haunts the room.

The woman was committed at the request of her husband because she was causing physical harm to herself. As the story goes, the woman was healthy and happy with a husband and children at home. She had long beautiful hair and seemed to have everything going for her. Then one day, for unknown reasons, she believed she was no longer attractive, and that her husband did not love her anymore. She became obsessed with her looks and stood in front of a mirror constantly brushing and pulling out her hair. With no other choice, her husband was forced to have her committed.

During her confinement at the manor, staff would find the woman standing in front of the mirror in her room, combing and pulling out her hair. Some paranormal enthusiasts who have visited the manor have recorded a woman's voice in the room, while others have witnessed the door opening and closing on its own. Later, you will read about two incidents that happened during our investigation to intern Lauren. The incidents took place at the opposite end of the hallway and may be connected to the spirit of the woman in room seven.

When our tour of the shadow man hallway was finished, we headed to the second floor to continue our walkthrough of the building. I always approach investigations of locations where a fee is required to investigate, with a healthy skepticism. But it was during our walkthrough of the second floor, I began to believe that Malvern Manor was the real deal.

After climbing the stairs to the second floor, Kurt stopped our group and said that there was something he wanted to tell us before the tour proceeded. *"Before we go any further,"* Kurt announced. *"I want to disclose that something will happen to at least one of you when we enter a particular room on the second floor, I guarantee it. To prove what I am saying, I will take one of you to the side beforehand, and tell them which room and what will happen, without telling the others."*

"This should be good," I thought to myself skeptically.

Kurt selected Bondsy as the one to confide the information to. Then we proceeded with the tour of the second floor. At the top of the stairs, the first room on the right side is a small inconspicuous room, known as Hanks room. Kurt explained that a patient named Hank who had a penchant for violence toward women, including the nursing staff, had once lived.

I felt nothing out of the ordinary in the room, but without prompting, Bondsy asked intern Lauren, *"Why are you holding your stomach?"*

To which she replied, *"Because I have pains in my stomach!"*

"How long have you had them," he questioned. *"They just started,"* Lauren replied.

"My stomach hurts too," added intern Kate. *"But I think it's because of the ranch dressing I had on my dinner salad that didn't agree with me."*

After Kurt finished talking about Hank, we exited the room. When we entered the hallway, Bondsy asked the group to stop before proceeding with the tour. He then asked the girls when they first noticed having stomach pains and both indicated the pains started as soon as they entered Hanks room. *"When Kurt pulled me aside, he told me one or more of us would come down with a stomachache in Hanks room,"* Bondsy explained.

"No way," exclaimed Lauren.

"Oh my," added Kate with a look of astonishment on her

face.

We all looked at each other in disbelief because none of us, except for Bondsy, knew this beforehand. It was at this moment, I started to believe the stories Kurt was telling us, were true. There were no chemicals or moldy smells to cause the sudden stomachaches that the girls had, and if something environmentally caused it, one would think it should have affected Bondsy and me as well, but it didn't.

The next room of importance that Kurt took us to, is one that intern Lauren would have several experiences in, Grace's room. Many ghosts have been experienced at Malvern Manor over the years, but none who haunt the building are more famous than Grace.

Grace was a patient who lived at the manor much of her life. She not only suffered from schizophrenia but was afflicted by multiple personality disorder. It is alleged that she had as many as fifty-six unique personalities. Staff often heard a man's voice coming from her room chanting, *"The Devil is coming to get me,"* which was repeated over and over in a gruff voice. But when the employees would enter her room, they discovered the voice was coming from Grace, as the man was just one of her many personalities. Grace's sunglasses and wheelchair are still in her room, giving the feeling that she still lives there. Later, you will read about events that took place in the room that affected Lauren.

Next, Kurt took us to the room, where young Inez Gibson was found hanging in her closet. While in the room, he told a story about a doll, that some believe is possessed. The doll is known as, *"Number One."* It was given this name, because a paranormal team, using the doll as a trigger mechanism to coax a response from the spirit of Inez, placed the doll on a dresser in her room. The group claimed that the doll flew off the dresser into the center of the room. When they reviewed audio from their recorder, they found they had recorded a voice they believe was the doll, saying, Number One!

The story doesn't end there. Kurt explained that more recent, people who have touched the doll have had bad things happen to them. He didn't allude to what happened, but said they now keep the doll in the office in a glass case. He took us to the office to see the doll. Kurt refused to touch it himself but indicated that if anyone wanted to hold it, we could take it out of the glass case and do so. Bondsy, Lauren and Kate declined, but me, being from the I have to see it to believe it, school of thought, said, *"Sure, I'll hold it."*

I felt confidant holding the doll, because Kurt held another doll he purchased from Costa Rica, that was advertised as being possessed. So, if Kurt held a possessed doll from Costa Rica, what harm could come from holding, Number One? Well, I would soon find out. Because less than twenty minutes after holding the doll, I fell from the top step of the attic to the bottom of the steps, causing a large bruise on my hip. So, the question is, was the fall the result of my clumsiness, or did Number One, play a role in my tumble down the steps? The jury is still out for me on this question. But before the night was over, several odd things took place, that may or may not be connected to Number One, which I will discuss a bit later in the chapter.

Introducing us to the doll was the last part of the tour, so Kurt headed out, leaving the manor to us for the night. The first thing we did was set up audio and video equipment throughout the building, then headed to the nurses wing and the shadow man hallway to begin the investigation.

Kurt's description of a shadowy figure following female investigators out of the hallway, and stories I read on the internet, portrayed the hallway as the center of the darkest activity. So, this part of the building was the logical choice to start our investigation.

Since the interns had never been on a paranormal investigation, we stayed together for the first part of the night. We headed down the first-floor hall to the nurses station, then turned left. On each side of the hall where rooms where patients once lived. At the end of the hallway was a locked exit door. In front of the door was an old bedpan and a cushioned seat or ottoman. It is important to note, that the tile floor at this end of the hallway, was clear of debris. So, there was nothing to obstruct our path as we walked down the hall. The importance of this will be apparent soon.

We didn't have an actual game plan for investigating the shadow man hallway, but after a few minutes of discussion between Bondsy and I, and a few more minutes to reassure the interns we would be nearby, we came up with a plan.

Based on Kurt's story of the shadow man following a group of female investigators down the hall, it seemed logical that if the shadow man were to show himself to anyone, it would be to female interns. So, after convincing the interns to be bait for a paranormal trap of sorts, our plan was to leave the girls at this end of the hall, while surveilling them from the opposite end of the hallway. We would only be one-hundred feet away and the girls were in range of our flashlights. So, if anything happened, we could get to the girls in a matter of seconds.

First I brushed off the ottoman with my hand to clear any dust off. The interns then sat next to each other, with Kate to Laurens right. For reassurance, Kate latched onto Lauren's right arm while Lauren held a flashlight. After confirming that the girls were ok with our plan, Bondsy and I headed to the opposite end of the hallway. When we reached our destination, I shined my flashlight toward the girls, and could see them in the obscure lighting. It wouldn't be long before the plan worked.

We could hear the girls whispering, when suddenly, Lauren called out in a nervous voice, *"Hey Larry!"* To which I replied. *"Is something wrong?"* *"Maybe,"* she responded. *"Something is playing with my hair!"*

"What," Bondsy questioned.

"Something just pulled my hair!"

"No way!" Bondsy replied.

"Larry, can you come down here?" Lauren asked in a nervous tone of voice.

"Sure," I said.

With that, we hurried down the hallway. When we got to the girls, Kate was acting strange. She was laughing and crying at the same time.

When I asked Lauren, who has long hair that was neatly pulled back in a ponytail, what happened. She said that she felt someone playing with her hair, then yank on it. I shined my flashlight on Lauren and saw a strand of hair sticking straight out on the left side of her head, or the opposite side from where Kate was sitting. It looked as though someone had pulled her hair.

She said she felt someone touching her hair, just before it was yanked. As you can imagine, the girls were a bit shaken by what happened. When they calmed down, Bondsy volunteered to sit on the ottoman, while the girls and I went to the other end of the hallway to see if anything would torment him like Lauren. While at the opposite end of the hall, I noticed a small yellow plastic ball about the size of a baseball. So that no one kicked it by accident, I placed it in the corner behind us. You will understand the relevance of my action, momentarily.

As we stood in silence monitoring Bondsy, all was quiet. Then, Bondsy asked, *"Did you guys hear that?"*

"No, what did you hear?" I responded.

"It sounded like a ball bouncing!" He explained in a perplexed tone of voice.

"No, I didn't hear anything," I said, moving toward Bondsy while shining my flashlight down the hall in his direction.

As I walked past the nurses station, the beam from my light lit up something in the middle of the hall approximately ten feet in front of Bondsy. *"Is that a ball in the middle of the floor,"* I questioned, pointing my light at what looked like a ping-pong ball in the middle of the hallway.

"No way," Bondsy said.

Next I heard, *"Oh my God,"* coming from one of the girls as they followed behind me, still on edge from the hair pulling incident.

"It is a ball," exclaimed Kate.

As I walked closer, I could see that it was a white ping-pong ball. One thing I am sure of, is there was nothing in the hallway when we walked from the ottoman to the opposite end of the hall a few minutes earlier. Now, sitting in the middle of the floor, was a ping-pong ball.

"That wasn't there before," Kate declared. *"No, it wasn't,"* Lauren added.

As we stood around the ball discussing how it got there, I asked Bondsy what the noise sounded like that he heard. *"It sounded like a ball bouncing, and now there is a ball in the middle of the floor that wasn't there before,"* he replied, raising his voice in excitement.

I picked up the ball and noticed it was flat on the bottom like it had been stepped on. So, there was no way it could have rolled or bounced to the center of the hallway.

"Ok," I said. *"It's my turn to set on the ottoman while you guys go to the other end of the hall."*

With that, Bondsy and the girls walked to the opposite end of the hall. I turned my flashlight on so I could find the ottoman in the darkness. When I did, I noticed a shiny penny laying on the right side of the ottoman. I remembered using my hand to brush the dust off the ottoman before the girls sat on it. So, I should have noticed the penny.

"Hey, do you guys remember seeing a shiny penny on the ottoman?" I questioned.

"What!" Bondsy asked in disbelief. *"There was no penny there,"* he continued."

The trio walked back toward me as I stood by the ottoman, the beam from my flashlight illuminating the penny.

"That was not there," Lauren said.

"No way," added Bondsy.

"I bet it fell out of your pocket, Bondsy," Kate proclaimed.

"It couldn't have," Bondsy retorted. *"I don't carry change. Remember back at the restaurant I told the waitress to keep the change. I don't like the feel of change in my pocket."*

After we all agreed that the shiny penny had not been on the ottoman, Bondsy and the girls once again headed to the opposite end of the hall, and I took a seat on the ottoman. Only a couple of minutes passed when I heard Bondsy and the girl's talking. It sounded like they were excited about something.

"Did you kick that ball, Bondsy," questioned a giggling Kate.

"No, I didn't," he replied.

"Oh shit, here we go again," exclaimed Kate, in a nervous voice.

"What's going on," I yelled out to the group.

"See that yellow ball over there on the other side of the hall," Bondsy asked, using the light from his flashlight as a spotlight. *"It just rolled out from behind us on its own and rolled down the hall."*

When Bondsy shined his light, I could see the ball he was referring to. It was the same ball that a few minutes earlier, I placed in the corner at the far end of the hall. I joined the group as they were gathered around the ball and asked them to show me where they were standing before it rolled.

They took a position three feet in front of the corner where I had placed the ball. The floor is level, so it could not have rolled on its own. If Bondsy or one of the girls kicked the ball, they would have had to kick their leg backwards, a distance of three feet, in order to touch the ball.

For whatever reason, someone, or something we couldn't see, seemed to be manipulating objects, and pulling hair in the shadow man hallway.

After taking a quick break, we headed to the second floor to continue our investigation. All was quiet, or so it seemed to be. Kate and I were walking ten feet in front of Lauren and Bondsy, when I heard a loud noise that sounded like someone kicked a door. I asked Kate if she heard the noise, and she did. Bondsy and Lauren didn't hear anything.

We checked the nearby rooms and found nothing out of the ordinary. But during audio review, I found two clear EVP's that were recorded after the commotion. The EVP sequence was recorded at 9:50 p.m. In the clip, you hear me asked Kate if she heard the noise to which she replies, *"Yeah!"* As soon as Kate responds to my question, a male voice, whispers, *"No!"*

Then, a second male voice says, *"Well Kate, you're not going to go prove it!"* It's speculation, but I believe the voice is telling Kate that she is not brave enough to go looking for the source of the noise. But regardless of what it may have meant, it knew her name.

Over the years, I have recorded my name being said, many times, even when investigating alone. Saying our names would seem to indicate that the recorded voices are intelligent and know who we are.

After heading back to the first floor, Kate needed to make a phone call to her college roommate, as class was starting in a few days after summer break. Since there was no cellphone signal inside, Kate went outside to make the call and Bondsy accompanied her for safety sake. While Bondsy and Kate were outside, Lauren and I headed back to the Shadow Man hallway to continue investigating. This time, I took a video camera equipped with infrared capabilities. We set up the camera near room seven at the opposite end of the hall and pointed it in the direction of the ottoman.

During casual conversation, I mentioned to Lauren I was disappointed I didn't have a camera pointed toward her when her hair was pulled. It surprised me when she volunteered to go by herself, and sit on the ottoman, while I monitored the camera. It surprised me, because it is unusual for someone who has never been on a paranormal investigation, to volunteer to do anything by themselves, let alone after having an experience like Lauren did.

After walking Lauren down the hallway, she sat on the ottoman, and I returned to the opposite end of the hall to monitor the camera. While surveilling her through the camera's viewfinder, I noticed a shadow behind Lauren but couldn't tell if it was her shadow or the shadow of someone or something else. I asked her to move her head back and forth, and then zoomed in on her using the telephoto lens. I could see it was Lauren causing the shadow.

After zooming in, I noticed Lauren fidgeting, then turn her flashlight on and look behind her. Before I could say anything, she called out. *"Hey Larry, something is touching my hair."*

"You're kidding," I responded.

"No, it just did it again and now something is pulling on my ponytail,"

Watching Lauren through the viewfinder, I zoomed in closer. No sooner than I did this, I saw Lauren's head violently snap back! *"Larry, can you come down here, something just yanked on my ponytail,"* Lauren shouted, with an urgent but semi-calm tone to her voice.

"Hang on, I'm on my way," I replied hurrying down the hall toward Lauren.

Surprisingly calm for having her hair yanked by a phantom hand, I asked her to describe what happened. She said it was similar to how her sister yanked on her hair when they were children. *"I felt something touching my hair, just before it yanked on my ponytail,"* she explained.

Soon after the incident, Bondsy and Kate rejoined us. After telling them what happened, we took a quick break outside, then headed to Grace's room to continue the investigation.

According to owner Kurt Fricke, Grace's room is one of the most paranormally active in the entire building. So, we were not sure what to expect after all the activity we had experienced in the Shadow Man hallway. We were standing around when Bondsy decided to sit in Grace's wheelchair to see if this would stimulate paranormal activity. It wasn't long before Bondsy was overcome with the feeling that he shouldn't be sitting in the chair.

He told me he couldn't put his finger on it, but he felt he needed to get out of the chair. I asked him if he felt like he was disrespecting Grace by sitting in her chair, and he replied, *"Yes, exactly!"*

As Bondsy got out of the chair, I thought to myself, *"Why not!"* Then took a seat in the wheelchair to see if I would get the same uncomfortable feeling, and I did. It was the same feeling of being disrespectful to Grace, so I got out of the chair as well.

When I exited the chair, Lauren commented that she was getting uncomfortably hot, which made little sense because we had been in other areas of the house that were even warmer. Plus, we had turned on the air conditioning in this part of the manor, so Grace's room was one of the cooler rooms we had been in.

No one else felt hot, so I shined my flashlight toward Lauren and sweat was rolling off her forehead. Before I could say anything else, she became sick to her stomach. *"I don't know what's wrong, but my stomach feels terrible,"* she said. *"It feels like I could throw up."*

Since Lauren wasn't feeling well, we headed to the kitchen, which was the coolest room in the manor. No sooner than we arrived in the kitchen, I noticed a long scratch on the left side of Lauren's neck. As I was examining the scratch, I had her turn and noticed a similar scratch on the right side of her neck as well.

"You probably scratched your neck with your fingernails," Bondsy interjected.

"No, I didn't," Lauren replied. *"Plus, I keep my nails cut short,"* she added, extending her hands showing us her neatly trimmed fingernails.

So far, all the unusual activity seemed to focus on Lauren, but why? Based on several conversations I had with her, combined with hearing her name whispered during our drive over to Malvern Manor, I wondered if Lauren was sensitive to spirits and may be what is called, empathic.

An empath is someone who senses the emotions of those around them, to the point of feeling the emotions themself. If you think about it, the manor is a place where patients and staff probably experienced the things that Lauren was experiencing on a daily basis. I'm sure there were times patients felt sick to their stomachs and times when they scratched themselves or staff and other patients.

We were in the kitchen discussing the possibility of Lauren being an empath when I realized something. At the opposite end of the shadow man hallway, and only a scant distance from where Lauren's hair was pulled, is room seven. If you remember, room seven is where a patient lived, who stood in front of a mirror, pulling out her hair. Could the phantom culprit that tugged on Lauren's hair be the ghost lady from room seven? Was she jealous of Lauren's hair and wanted to pull it out, or did she think it was beautiful and wanted to touch it?

I have been on a lot of paranormal investigations in twenty years, and the only time I have encountered someone getting their hair pulled, was at Malvern Manor. So, what are the odds of this occurring in a hallway where a woman's room is located, who pulled out her own hair? It makes sense, that if the ghost of the woman from room seven haunts her room, she may haunt the hallway as well, obsessed with hair even after death. After discussing the scratches and the possibility of the woman being the culprit who pulled Lauren's hair, we took a break outside, hoping Lauren's upset stomach would subside.

After a short fifteen-minute break, we returned to the kitchen area before continuing the investigation. It was at this time that something unusual happened to me. Bondsy approached me with a concern. It worried him that activity seemed to be escalating, especially with Lauren. *"First it was mild hair pulling, then a violent yank of her hair, then she felt sick, and now something scratched her,"* Bondsy said. *"Maybe we should wrap things up and call it a night."*

I'm not sure what happened, but I lost my temper and shouted at Bondsy which was out of character for me.

I said, *"You bring interns along hoping they get scared to make for good radio, then when things happen, you want to go home. You need to take the paranormal serious and understand it is not entertainment."* Bondsy tried to calm me down, but I walked away from him.

Did getting upset with Bondsy and falling down the attic stairs have anything to do with holding the alleged possessed doll? A few weeks after the investigation, I had a conversation with Bondsy about this topic. When I asked him if he thought the doll had anything to do with my sudden quick-temper or falling down the stairs, he told me he had talked with the interns about what happened, and they too wondered the same thing.

Bondsy also said he thought it was strange how both intern Kate and intern Lauren acted out of character during the investigation. He reminded me of how Kate reacted when Lauren's hair was pulled. How she was laughing and crying at the same time, which made little sense. *"On the other hand,"* he said. *"Lauren was calm during the night, even after having her hair violently pulled, getting sick to her stomach, and being scratched.* Bondsy said that Lauren has more of an anxious or timid personality, so it made little sense to him that these things didn't upset her. We may never know if the doll had anything to do with the way we acted, but it sure makes one wonder.

Since we had not investigated the attic, I headed up there on my own, while the group continued investigating downstairs. I was in the attic for an hour, and nothing happened. When I returned downstairs things were calm, so we decided to call it a night. The investigation was eventful, to say the least. I don't think the interns expected anything would happen, so to say they got more than they bargained for on their first paranormal investigation, is an understatement.

EVP Evidence

The following day, I began reviewing audio and video from our cameras and recorders. Based on the personal experiences we had, I hoped to find evidence of paranormal activity and as it turned out, was not disappointed. I should note that the only thing we heard during the investigation was the loud noise recorded at 9:49 p.m. All other EVP's were recorded, but not heard by our team.

9:49 p.m.

The first EVP recorded was the loud crashing sound that Kate and I heard while on the second-floor hallway. The only device that recorded the noise was a recorder we placed in an empty room on the first floor that Kurt indicated was a suitable location for recording EVP's. I can best describe what we recorded, as sounding like something heavy toppled over.

Upon checking the room where the noise was recorded and other nearby rooms, we could not determine the source of the commotion.

9:50 p.m.

The next EVP I found, was discussed earlier in the chapter. After hearing the loud crashing sound on the second floor, I asked Kate if she heard it, to which she acknowledged she did. It was during this time, that the audio recorder in the first-floor room, recorded a whisper, followed by a voice that seemed to interact with the conversation Kate and I were having. When I asked Kate if she heard the noise, and she responded yes. A voice whispers, *"no,"* and for all intents and purposes, seemed to be mocking my question. Immediately after the whisper, a male voice says, *"Well Kate, you're not going to go prove it!"*

Who or whatever is speaking, knows Kate's name and one could infer that the phantom voice is saying that it knows Kate will not go looking for the source of the noise. Somehow, the phantoms behind the voices I record, know who we are. Which leads me to believe that even though invisible to us, they are nearby and can hear our conversations.

10:46 p.m.
Unfortunately, only part of the fourth EVP of the night is distinct. The voice is male, and says, *"Get,"* followed by what sounds like either *"her"* or *"them."* We recorded the voice in the parlor. No matter if the voice is saying, *"get her or get them,"* the statement infers that it is talking to someone else.

10:55 p.m.
EVP number five was recorded at 10:55 p.m., and EVP number six recorded at 11:40 p.m., which you will read about shortly. Both sound like the same voice, and sound like someone is disguising their voice. Both EVP's were recorded in the room on the first floor that Kurt advised was an excellent location for recording unexplained phenomena. The voice talks in a high-pitched voice reminiscent of the cartoon character, Mickey Mouse. The voice says, *"Hey, did you hear that?"* I'm not sure what the ghostly voice is referring to, because we heard nothing at the time we recorded it.

11:40 p.m.
The last unexplained voice of the night was clear, and again sounded like the high pitched, Mickey Mouse sounding voice recorded at 10:55 p.m. It is a beckoning voice that asks, *"Where are you?"*

The Mickey Mouse sounding voices, sounded like someone trying to disguise their voice. Remembering the stories of Grace and how she would disguise her own voice, I wondered if the recorded voices were her.

Malvern Manor was definitely worth the long drive from central Illinois. Whatever is there is not shy when it comes to interacting with the living and is a place I hope to spend more time in the future.

I believe the reason the activity was focused on Lauren is because she is sensitive to spirits. After all, if a ghost wants to interact with the living, who better to reach out to, than someone who can sense they are there.

But regardless of whether you are sensitive to spirits or not, doesn't seem to matter at Malvern Manor. Because even someone like me, who couldn't sense a spirit if they were sitting on my lap, can tell there is something ghostly lurking in the shadows and hallways of the manor. Something that, for whatever reason, chooses to remain after death and interact with the living. Malvern Manor was definitely a trip I will not forget anytime soon and is a place that someday I hope to return to.

Kansas

SALLIE HOUSE

SEVEN

Prior to becoming a paranormal investigator, I read books, heard stories, watched movies and documentaries about places such as the Sallie House. But the problem with reading books and watching movies is you can never be sure what you are reading or watching is real or actually took place. So, for this reason, I have to see these things for myself.

My September 14, 2013, investigation would be my second investigation at the Sallie House. The first was the previous year and was conducted on May 30, 2012, with paranormal investigator Jay. Jay had accompanied me on other investigations, but there was something about the Sallie House that truly bothered him, especially when we made our way down to the basement. He didn't like it down there, which was completely out of character for him.

Jay was the type of investigator, who usually looked forward to investigating what most would consider the creepiest part of a location. The basement is usually the first place that he will head to. The Sallie House was different; Jay couldn't wait until we would leave the basement and go back upstairs to the main part of the house to investigate. But even then, he was very uncomfortable in the house. Never before had I seen Jay react this way and he hasn't reacted in this manner since. To this day he refuses to go back to the house because he knows the risk, and something is telling him that the risk is not worth the reward.

During the 2012 investigation, we recorded several unusual

EVP's, some of which were children's voices. One clearly says, *"I'll quit,"* while another says either, *"Mikey"* or *"my key,"* followed by several additional words that I haven't been able to decipher. I also recorded a voice that sounds like a young girl speaking who simply says, *"I'm coming!"*

I decided to conduct the September 2013 investigation alone for two reasons. The first reason was, I wouldn't have to be concerned about the safety of anyone else. The second reason; by investigating alone, there wouldn't be any other voices in the house. So, when I reviewed my audio and video recordings, any voices recorded other than my own, would leave little doubt they were paranormal in nature. Which would be evidence that the place is haunted.

I found out about the Sallie house while watching an episode of the Discovery Channel's, *A Haunting*, television series in the fall of 2006. The episode was about a young Kansas couple, Tony, and Debra Pickman, who were newlyweds, and had just moved into what would be their first house together. They were expecting their first child, but what they didn't expect was the unexplained and frightening events that would soon take place. Events that take place to this day, still haunting the Pickman's, even though they no longer live in the house.

Soon after their son Taylor was born, strange events began happening in the house. Lights would turn on and off, candles would light by themselves, and toy dolls, along with stuffed animals, would move on their own.

Eventually Tony saw the ghost of a little girl. He first saw her in the kitchen of the house as he was getting a glass of juice from the refrigerator. When he closed the refrigerator door, he saw a little girl standing in the kitchen. Tony told me his first thought was, *"How did the neighbor's child get inside my house?"* Then he noticed something that caused him to drop the glass of juice he was holding. He noticed that he could see through the little girl and could see the cabinets that were behind her. As you can imagine, this was very unnerving to Tony.

The Sallie House

Tony was the only one who ever saw the ghost child. A psychic medium who investigated the house sensed the presence of a child's spirit named Sallie, haunting the Pickman's home. Another psychic who later investigated the house also sensed the presence of a little girl named Sallie. The second psychic investigator did this, without having prior knowledge of the name that the first psychic came up with.

A neighbor who had heard about the unusual activity going on, and who had once lived in the house, told the Pickman's that while she lived there, her daughter had an invisible playmate, who she called Sallie. The woman had no prior knowledge that the psychic mediums, also mentioned the name of a little girl named Sallie. From that point on, the house was known as, Sallie's House or the Sallie House.

Many stories have been told over the years of things that allegedly happened, causing the house to be haunted. Unfortunately, none of the stories have been confirmed. One such story talked about a desperate mother who brought her ill child, named Sallie, to see a doctor who lived in the house at 508 N. Second Street. According to the legend, the mother brought the child, sick with pneumonia to the doctor in the middle of the night. As the story goes, the doctor had to perform emergency surgery on the child and did so without using anesthetic. The little girl died during the painful and horrifying ordeal. It is said that she takes out her vengeance of what happened to her by haunting the house.

When I spoke to the Pickman's, they told me that in the many hours of research that they have done, they have never found any evidence to validate the story about the little girl dying in the house. They have been able to verify through records that at one time, a doctor, his mother, and a sister occupied the residence, but due to the relatively small size of the house, it is doubtful the doctor had his medical practice there.

The haunting activity the Pickman's experienced began slowly. Occasionally, their television, as well as other electrical devices, would turn on and off by themselves, even when no one was around. Pictures on the wall would be turned upside down. Tony would straighten the pictures only to come back later and find them upside down again.

They tried to rationalize the events, as most would do, and blamed the strange activity on things such as outdated wiring or their own forgetfulness. When their son, Taylor, was born, the activity seemed to pick up even more. One of the events that I always remember from the television show, was a time when Debra's sister was visiting after the baby was born.

One night, Tony was upstairs, and something caught his eye in the baby's nursery. When he went into the room, he noticed how all of the stuffed animals had been moved from the shelves where they were normally kept and had been arranged in a circle on the floor of the nursery. Tony called to his wife and sister-in-law to come upstairs to see the strange arrangement on the floor. When they saw how the toys were arranged, the sisters couldn't believe their eyes and actually thought Tony was playing a joke on them. He was finally able to convince them that he had nothing to do with arranging the toys in this manner.

Tony's brother, who was a practical joker, lived near the house. He became the prime suspect and was blamed for moving the stuffed animals. The Pickman brothers enjoyed playing pranks on each other, but Tony and Deb, couldn't figure out how he could have got in the house, without anyone seeing or hearing him.

The trio placed the stuffed animals back on the shelves where they had originally been and headed back downstairs. A few minutes later, Tony went upstairs and as he passed by the nursery, something again caught his attention. When he stopped and looked in the room, he couldn't believe what he was seeing. Because the toys, were again arranged in a circle and placed on the floor.

As time went on, things became more malevolent with objects, such as candles and toys, bursting into flames. Then physical things started happening to Tony. Deep scratches would form on his body out of nowhere, and his clothing would spontaneously burst into flames. He began having nightmares. The dreams were vivid, and bizarre in nature. In the dreams, Tony would hear strange words repeated over and over. Words, that didn't make sense to him. He could only recall one specific word after having the dreams.

Renowned psychic Peter James, who worked for the TV series *Sightings,* investigated the house. James, who passed away several years ago, was one of the most highly respected psychics in the field of paranormal research. He told Tony, that one of the entities haunting the house, was a demon, who was causing all of the negative activity. James identified the demon by name, and that name was *Belial!* When he was told this, he was in shock, because the only word he could understand or remember from the nightmares, was the name,

Belial.

After years of paranormal research, I am finding a pattern of two common denominators, among cities and towns having an unusually high number of locations reported to be haunted. Most of them are located on or near a river. Atchison, Kansas, Hannibal, Missouri, Quincy and Alton, Illinois, are among cities reported to be the most haunted cities in America and are all located near major rivers. The second common denominator, is all of the towns, are located on hills with an abundance of limestone. Limestone is prevalent both in the natural terrain as well as in the architecture of the buildings and landscape surrounding the cities. It seems the combination of water and limestone, is present in a majority of hauntings, especially in cases of extreme hauntings.

Limestone is known to have large deposits of the mineral quartz in it. Quartz transmits ultraviolet or short light waves better than glass. Ultraviolet light can be detected by many animals including dogs and cats. I have had numerous witnesses having paranormal activity going on in their homes, tell me that their cat or dog will stare at or follow something with their eyes, while the witness see's nothing. So, it is possible, ghosts and phantoms dwell in the ultraviolet spectrum, which may be why many times, people sense someone, or something is there, but see nothing.

The history of Atchison is very interesting. It is located forty-five minutes northwest of the Kansas City metro area, forty minutes northeast of the capitol city of Topeka, and twenty-five minutes southwest of St. Joseph, Missouri. The land, where Atchison is located, was once home to the Kansa Indians. They made their home near the plentiful land by the Missouri river. After the explorers, Lewis, and Clark, departed from St. Louis, in May of 1804, on what was the first American expedition to the now western portion of the United States, they found what remained of the Kansa village. On July 20th, 1854, Atchison, named for David Rice Atchison, a noted

Missouri senator, became one of the first towns in the Kansas territory. For many years it was a thriving commercial hub. Mostly, due to its access to the Missouri River, and the establishing of steamboat landings near the town. In the early years, as many as four or five steamboats, landed daily at Atchison on their travels between St. Louis and St. Joseph, Missouri.

The town continued to thrive as the Overland Stage Line and Salt Lake City-based freighters made it the end of their travel route to the east. The stagecoach line traveled from Atchison to Placerville, Calif, making it one of the longest and most important routes in the country. The U.S. Post Office established Atchison as its headquarters and was the starting point for mail heading west. When the boom days of overland trade started to die out in the 1860s, Atchison's leaders set their focus on developing the city as a railroad hub. A $150,000 investment from local leaders, led to the forming of the Atchison, Topeka & Santa Fe Railroad. Even with delays caused by the Civil War, the rail line continued to expand in Atchison. By 1872, the Chicago, Rock Island & Pacific Railroad arrived, making it the eighth different railroad line which used Atchison as a terminal. Four of these connected to the Missouri side.

At the beginning of the 20th century, the Topeka Mail & Breeze described Atchison as having more rich men and widows in proportion to its population than any other city in Kansas. These wealthy citizens-built scores of grand mansions, many of which still stand today. Failing to build a bridge over the Missouri River until 1875 put Atchison ten years behind cities such as Kansas City and St. Joseph, Missouri. This led to the decline in prosperity and expansion of commercial ventures.

Not far from the Sallie house, aviator Amelia Earhart was born in her grandparent's home, where she lived during her childhood. The city survived two flash floods that swept through the downtown area in the 1880s and became known as, *"The city that refused to die."* Unfortunately, the floods washed away many of the records of the land where the Sallie House sits, limiting research on the property. Ironically, much like Atchison itself, the house seems to refuse to die as well.

I have several social media pages on the web, including a personal Facebook page, as well as one for my paranormal interest under *Urban Paranormal Investigations*. Many, of my friends follow me on these pages, as they are interested in my paranormal investigations and endeavors. So, when I decided to do the Sallie House investigation alone, I posted several messages and photos, to keep my friends updated on what was happening.

At one point, I posted a photo of the basement of the Sallie house on the Facebook page. It was a photo of a large hole in the basement wall. The hole is located just to the right and behind the stairs in the basement. I posted a message along with the photo, saying how this particular wall gives me a very bad vibe and for some reason makes me uneasy.

I have met people in my years as a paranormal investigator, who claim they are gifted and have psychic abilities. Only a hand full of those claiming to be gifted, have proved to me they are legitimate psychics. Two of these people are friends that I met through the paranormal community. One is a musician named Sam and the other named Felicia, was serving in the armed forces at the time.

After posting the photo of the hole in the basement wall, and describing the bad feeling I was getting, a few moments later, I received a private message from Sam. In Sam's message, he explained to me, how he didn't feel anything unusual, when looking at the photo of the wall with the hole in it. In the message, he said, *"Larry, the wall that you need to be concerned with, is the wall directly across from the wall with the hole in it."* I responded to Sam thanking him for his insight and told him that I would make sure to be on my guard in this area of the basement.

Less than ten minutes after receiving the message from Sam, I received a private message from Felicia, who was stationed at a military base in Korea. I should point out, that neither Sam nor Felicia have ever met, are not Facebook friends and as far as I know, don't know each other. The message that I received from Felicia was also about the photo of the hole in the basement wall. Felicia told me the exact same thing that Sam had messaged me.

In addition, Felicia warned me about something else in the house that I should be aware of. In her message, she said, *"Larry, I keep seeing you finding a folded rope in the house. If you find one, do not touch it as there is danger associated with it!"* When people like Sam and Felicia warn me about something, I pay close attention to them, because they have been extremely accurate in their psychic visions before.

On Saturday September 14th, I headed out on the five-and-a-half-hour drive to Atchison from my home in Taylorville, Illinois. It was a mostly sunny day, and the drive was without incident. Before I continue, I should explain that since I have been investigating the paranormal, at times while preparing for an investigation, or talking about my investigations to groups or when doing radio and TV interviews, unusual things happen, including electronic and mechanical equipment malfunctioning. This has happened many times.

An example of this was when I was doing a live on-air interview with Chad Douglas of CBS station KHQA in Quincy, Illinois. Chad's lead into my interview that morning was a promo for the movie *Paranormal Activity III*, which at the time, was a new movie release. Although exaggerated by Hollywood, the movie did parallel some of the things I have seen and experienced myself, so it was a good lead in for my interview.

Chad began by asking general questions about paranormal investigating, and I discussed some of the haunted sites in the book that were local to the viewing area of the station. I discussed nearby Hannibal, Missouri and a place called Rockcliffe Mansion. After discussing the mansion, Chad asked if I had ever experienced anything more extreme, such as what was shown in the movie promo for Paranormal Activity. I explained that yes, I had experienced similar things after returning home from an investigation at the Villisca Axe Murder house in Iowa.

In particular, one of the things I talked about was how mechanical and electronic equipment would break down when I was around. How it was not an occasional occurrence, but something that happened all of the time and no matter where I went. The interview lasted about four and a half minutes and once we were finished, a producer and a technician came out from the control room and approached us.

The producer asked Chad, if we were finished with the interview, because they wanted to talk to me. Chad indicated we were finished, and she began explaining how strange things happened as soon as I mentioned that mechanical, and electronic equipment, malfunctioned when I was around.

She further explained, that as soon as I said this, a variety of technical problems occurred in the control room. Problems like the overhead lights flickering on and off, audio equipment and video monitors stopped working, computers malfunctioned and not just network computers, but personal laptops as well. *"In all the years I've worked in the studio, this has never happened,"* she said.

Continuing with her story she explained that once my interview was over, the equipment began to function normally again. *"To say the crew were spooked by what happened, would be an understatement,"* she said. *"There may have been skeptics in the studio when you arrived for the interview,* but *there are a whole lot of believers* now."

Unusual things happened soon after arriving in Atchison as

well. I decided beforehand when I arrived, I would stop at a gas station to fill up. This way, I wouldn't have to stop for gas in the morning before heading home. When I pulled into the station and got out of my vehicle, I noticed a sign on the fuel pump that read, *"Pre-pay inside."*

So, I walked into the station and stood behind two customers who were in line. As I was waiting, the clerk behind the counter announced, *"I'm sorry folks, but our computers just went down, so it will be twenty to thirty minutes before they are back up."* Rather than wait, I decided to head down the highway to see if I could find another gas station. I drove a few miles and pulled into another station. Once again when I got out of my car, there was a sign on the pump, which read: *Pre-pay, please pay inside!*

I entered the store and approached the clerk at the counter. *"Forty dollars on pump four please,"* I said. The clerk started to ring up the forty dollars on the register, but suddenly stopped.

He looked at me and said, *"I'm sorry sir, but my computer just went down, so it will be a few minutes before I can authorize the pump."* Not wanting to wait, I headed on to the Sallie House, and decided that I would fuel up later. I didn't think much about what happened, because being in a small town, both stations may have been using the same internet provider. But I did find it odd that the computer at the second station was working when I arrived, because if they were using the same internet service it should have already been down when I walked in.

When I scheduled the Sallie House investigation, with Les the owner, he told me the Chamber of Commerce was doing an afternoon tour at the house, but I could get into the house at 4:00 p.m. When I arrived at the house, it was 3:15 p.m., and a car was parked in front of the house. Figuring it was the tour guide's car and since I was early, I decided to get out of my car and take a few photos of the house. I was standing on the sidewalk in front of the house when I heard someone singing. I turned to my right, and a quarter of a block away, was a little boy, probably nine or ten years old, riding his bike down the sidewalk I was standing on. He was headed in my direction, so I moved forward and watched him as he came closer. I smiled at him as he passed me on the sidewalk. As my eyes followed him, I saw his bike come to a complete stop, as if he had hit something, and the little boy went flying over the handlebars. He quickly got up and brushed himself off but had a puzzled look on his face. I asked him if he was alright, and he indicated he was.

I walked over to the spot where he fell but didn't see anything that would have caused him to fall. It was like he hit an invisible barrier. Knowing the reputation of the house, I wondered if the boy falling was in some way connected to the haunting, and possibly a message to me. Or was it simply my imagination getting the best of me. With the Sallie House, anything is possible.

A third unusual thing happened before the investigation. Each weekend, I attend mass on Saturday evening, so I drove across town to attend services at St. Joseph's Catholic Church. I usually sit somewhere in the back of the church, so I found a seat next to the isle in the last few rows. When the processional started and the priest walked by me, his robe brushed my shoulder. Shortly after the opening hymn was finished, the priest started to speak in order to begin mass. However, his microphone malfunctioned, so only the congregation in the first few rows could hear what he was saying for the duration of the mass.

Were the incidents, in which computers malfunctioned at two separate gas stations, the little boy's bike suddenly and unexpectedly stopping causing him to go flying over the handlebars, and now the priest's microphone not working, somehow related to the Sallie House and my investigation? Or were they simply coincidental, unrelated to anything, other than electronic malfunction and carelessness. For those of you who know me, you know that coincidence is not an option for me.

After mass, I headed back to the house to get ready for the investigation. When I arrived, I unloaded my equipment, and carried it into the dining room area of the house. Once everything was inside, I conducted a walk-through to plan out where I would set up my audio and video recording equipment. During the walk-through, I used an EMF detector, and an infrared thermometer, to see if there were any unusual temperature or magnetic field fluctuations in the house or basement. I randomly checked this throughout the night, and there were no drastic changes.

When I entered the kitchen, I noticed that the door leading to the basement was open. Hanging in the middle of the doorway, was a paper sign that was blocking the staircase. On the sign were the words, *"No One Beyond This Point."*

The sign was hanging from a rope tied to the doorknob of the basement door, then strung across and tied to a galvanized pipe being used as a railing for the staircase. I thought to myself, *"I didn't drive six hours, to not investigate the creepiest part of the house, the basement!"* So, I untied the rope from the handrail, and headed down the wooden steps to the cellar.

I flipped the light switch, but it wasn't working, so I used my flashlight to see as I walked down the steps. What I didn't realize was one of the steps was broken. When my foot landed on the step, it wobbled, causing me to lose my balance. Almost falling, I grabbed the railing to steady myself and regain my balance.

I looked around the basement for a few minutes and placed an audio recorder on a metal folding chair then headed back up the stairs, stepping over the broken step. I was looking for electrical outlets in the kitchen to plug my DVR and surveillance system into, when my eyes were drawn to the basement door and in particular, the sign hanging from it.

What I *noticed* was the sign was attached to a long *rope*. A rope that had been folded in half, wrapped around the doorknob, then tied to the railing. Then I remembered what my psychic friend Felicia said to me in her message. *"Larry, I keep seeing you finding a folded rope in the house. If you find it, don't touch it, as there is danger associated with it!"*

The Sign

Then I thought about the broken step and how I had almost fallen because of it. *"The broken step was definitely dangerous,"* I thought to myself. Because if someone stumbled and fell, like I almost did, they could easily injure themselves. Or was the danger something else lurking in the shadows of the basement? Felicia's vision turned out to be accurate. So, now you see why I pay attention to what my clairvoyant friends say.

The next hour was spent setting up audio and video equipment. When I finished, I was scheduled to meet with

Tony and Deb at their home. The Pickman's, who experienced one of the most extreme hauntings ever reported, still live in Atchison, only eight blocks from the Sallie House. Unfortunately, simply moving out of the house did not stop the strange goings on, as unusual activity takes place in their current home. Much of the activity occurs when people like me, investigate the house. During my previous investigation, Tony told me, he knows when paranormal groups investigate the house and do things they shouldn't, like taunting or provoking. He knows this because activity increases in his own home.

So, it seems, hauntings, and especially this particular haunting, are not limited by walls, property lines or street addresses. Brick, mortar, wood, and distance do not prevent supernatural things from following you when they want to.

I have a lot in common with the Pickman's in that we have had similar experiences at the same places, in particular, the Villisca Ax Murder House in Iowa and the Sallie House in Atchison. I won't go into detail about what happened to me after I came home from the Villisca House in September of 2008 and again in October of 2010, as this was covered extensively in my book, *"Where Evil Lurks."* Deb and Tony became paranormal investigators after their Sallie House experience and one of the places they investigated, was the Villisca House. Their experiences related to the Villisca House, were similar to mine, so whenever we get together, we have a lot to talk about.

When I arrived at the Pickman's house, Tony was in the front yard with another gentleman, who was looking at a Halloween prop created by Tony. Tony is a fantastic artist and has a small business called *Bizoddities* in which he hand makes Halloween props out of synthetic materials. Believe me when I say his creations are Hollywood level, in terms of realism and quality. Much like my previous visit with the Pickman's, we chatted for several hours. Our conversations are always interesting, and time passes quickly. This time however, I witnessed something mind boggling.

I had read stories and seen photos of Tony who claimed to have been scratched by an unseen force while living in the Sallie House and at his current home. As I mentioned, this usually happens when someone is investigating the house or when Tony is discussing the haunting with someone.

The scratches may have something to do with Tony developing clairvoyance while living in the Sallie House. He is not sure how it happened, it just miraculously developed. I have witnessed his psychic abilities firsthand several times and they are nothing short of amazing.

We were seated at the dining room table. Tony was giving me advice about something I needed to do before I went back to the house for the investigation. While we were talking, he seemed uncomfortable and flinched, then mentioned how he was feeling a burning sensation on his stomach and chest. He lifted up his shirt and sure enough, there were scratches. He didn't seem too concerned, and my first thought was he could have scratched himself before I arrived. But my presumption soon changed, when right before my eyes, I witnessed scratches forming while his shirt was raised. It was amazing and freakish at the same time!

It looked like an invisible cat was clawing his skin. I told Tony I didn't want to cause him any grief by investigating the house, so if he preferred I cancel my investigation, I would do so and come back another time. Smiling, he said, *"Oh, no problem, this isn't bad. I've had much worse happen."* Seeing the scratches forming was additional proof for me of how real the supernatural and what goes on at the Sallie House is!

After visiting with the Pickman's for several hours, I returned to the Sallie House to start my investigation. I took precautions by preparing myself through prayer, before re-entering the house. Even after doing this, when I walked through the door, it had a different feel to it than it had earlier in the day. It was a heavy feeling, almost one of dread. Maybe I was on edge and more alert entering a house that was now dark, and one with a reputation of being a place of pure evil.

It was very warm inside, because I shut all the windows to keep outside noise from interfering with my audio equipment I left recording while visiting the Pickman's. Not only was it warm, it felt like someone was watching me. Adding to this feeling, all night long I heard movement in the upstairs and the basement, but when I would go to investigate, nothing was there. It was like something was playing games and trying to unnerve me.

During the night, I had a strong feeling, especially when in the basement, that something was down there, and possibly several *somethings*. The only other place I have had this feeling, was the Villisca house.

Psychic Peter James identified a portal to another realm in the back corner of the dining room. The owner of the house told me this when I investigated in 2012. So, I decided to use copper rods to test for unusual fields of energy in the spot identified as the portal. The use of copper rods in detecting energy fields is similar to the use of divining rods to locate water. Many paranormal investigators, believe the rods act as a conductor for energy sources that spirits can manipulate. So, if they can manipulate energy fields, the theory is, they can manipulate the rods to respond to yes or no questions. Although not completely sold on the reliability of copper rods in the detection of energy fields, I had used them several times at other locations, with success, so, I decided to give them a try in the dining room.

I wasn't disappointed, because when I held the rods in the location of the alleged portal, they began spinning in opposite directions of each other, then reversed direction. Using my EMF detector, I checked the area where they reacted, and no unusual electromagnetic readings were detected. Whether a portal or not, the rods spinning indicated something was going on in that spot. The water was disconnected, so it was doubtful they were detecting a water line.

Two other rooms in the house gave me a feeling I needed to be on guard, and that was Tony and Deb's old bedroom and the kitchen. I'm not sure what it was about the rooms, but for some reason they just felt off.

Most of the night was uneventful, but the house tends to keep you on edge. It's not simply the reputation of the place, there is more to it. Several times during the night, it felt like someone was in a nearby room watching, but when I would go check, there was no one there

I saved the creepiest area of the house for last. So, from 3:00 a.m. to 5:00 a.m., I investigated the basement. It's hard to describe the feeling it gives you, but there is a strong feeling that something is not right, and you just want to get out of there.

The first time I investigated the house, I noticed a spot on the basement floor, that was painted over with black paint. Tony told me that Les the owner, painted over the spot on the floor, when he discovered a tenant painted a pentagram on the floor and was practicing black magic. From what I was told, the tenant was asked to move.

During the last two decades, I have investigated a lot of places with basements, but there is something about the Sallie House basement that is different than all the others. When you turn the lights off, an unnerving feeling of dread and apprehension fills your body.

I placed two cameras and an audio recorder in the basement. One pointed toward the staircase, and one set up next to the wall that Sam and Felicia identified as the one I should be wary of and pointed it toward me. There were two metal folding chairs located against the wall directly across from the stairs. I placed an audio recorder on one chair, and I sat in the other. When I was ready to begin the basement investigation, I turned off my flashlight and placed it on the floor near me. As the light turned off, the basement became a dark abyss, with the only source of light the reflection from the LCD screen of the video camera next to the wall. The reflection of light was like a beacon, serving as a reference point in the darkness and a bit of comfort as well. But even at that, it was so dark, I couldn't see my hand in front of my face.

Investigating the Sallie House basement alone in the dark, is one of the most uncomfortable feelings I have had since investigating the paranormal. Afterall, I was alone in the dark, in a place identified by a gifted psychic like Peter James, as having a demonic presence. It felt like any moment something was going to reach out and grab me.

I began an EVP session in hopes of hearing or recording a response. Little did I expect with the first question I asked, whatever was down there, would let me know, that *"Yes, I'm here!"*

When I said, *"If there are any spirits or beings present, say something, or make a noise to let me know you are here."* No sooner than I uttered the words, *"let me know,"* the camera next to the wall, shut down. The reflection of the cameras LCD screen was my only source of light, so I couldn't see anything. My heart was pounding, because I knew there was no reason for the camera to shut off, as half of the four-hour battery charge was left.

When the camera shut down, it felt like I was sitting in a room full of people and at any moment, something would reach out and grab me. Adding to the intensity of the moment, was the eerie silence that filled the room.

Trying to keep my composure, I reached for my flashlight but couldn't find it. Feeling around the dark floor, I finally located it, but hesitated turning it on, because it felt like someone was standing directly in front of me, and if something was there, I wasn't sure I wanted to see what it was. Pressing the button on the end of the flashlight was one of the most unnerving things I have ever done, not knowing who or what would be standing in front of me when the light came on.

Finally, I pressed the button, and the light came on, but nothing, was there! Even though I didn't see anything, the hair stood up on the back of my neck, and I still felt the presence. Was it Belial, Sallie, or some other entity in the house, or was it just my imagination?

Walking over to the camera, I closed the LCD screen as it also serves as the power switch for the camera. When I reopened the screen, the camera powered on. The battery meter indicated that I still had 117 minutes of 240 minutes of battery remaining. Pressing the record button, the camera started recording and continued recording until the battery drained well over an hour later.

Did the camera simply malfunction or did something paranormal cause the camera to turn off? I'm not sure, but this never happened before, and has not happened since. My gut feeling is something was letting me know they were there, and shutting the camera off, may have been a sign of its presence.

I continued with the EVP session and spent the remainder of the night in the basement without incident. Maybe I passed some kind of test, and the presence decided that I wasn't worth the effort to try and scare. I can honestly say, there is a fine line between faith and fear, and fortunately, faith prevailed, allowing me to complete the investigation.

When 5:00 a.m. rolled around and since nothing else had happened, I decided to pack up and head home. After returning home to Taylorville, I began reviewing the more than forty hours of audio and forty hours of video I had recorded. Not having anyone with me during the investigation, made reviewing evidence easier. By investigating alone, the only voice I should have recorded, is that of my own when conducting EVP sessions, but that wasn't the case. Because when I began reviewing audio, I couldn't believe what I heard. Not only had I recorded my voice while conducting EVP sessions, but other voices as well, even during the time I was visiting with the Pickman's and not in the house. Which means, voices were recorded in a locked house, that no one else had access to, while I was at the Pickman's.

I also recorded strange voices in the house, that were recorded when I was not speaking or asking questions. Some are hard to understand, while others are clear, and some sound negative or threatening. I didn't physically hear any of the voices when they were recorded.

One voice, makes a statement, asks a question, then answers the question. What the voice says can be taken several ways! In the EVP sequence I refer to, you hear a whispery voice say, *"The one,"* immediately followed by the same voice saying, *"He's the one?"* As if it is asking a question. Next, the voice says, *"Right!"* Like they are confirming that the person, they are talking about is the one. My question is, is the person they are talking about, me?

The second EVP I recorded, is a voice that says, *"He must come home with you!"* Whenever I listen to this EVP, it sends a cold chill down my spine. Because if it is an intelligent entity, I may be the focus of the conversation, and if I am, is it saying that something must come home with me, or that I must go home with something in the house.

The third EVP is equally as unnerving as the previous one. It says, *"Come see, Come seek"*, then the voice whispers *"Deliver!"* This one is a bit confusing to me, as it didn't seem to make a lot of sense at first. The recording sounds like two voices talking and once again, I wonder if I was the focus of the conversation.

EVP number four was recorded in the living room. There is

no doubt who the voice is referring to in this clip because it says, *"Go back Larry."* So, was a spirit looking out for me or was something simply telling me to leave?

During the May 2012 investigation, I recorded several EVP's of children. One voice, sounds like a young girl, saying, *"Mikey* or *My Key!"* I bring up the clip, because during the 2013 investigation, I recorded a similar sounding little girl or child saying, *"All done Mom!"* The voice speaks in such a matter-of-fact way, I doubt it even knew I was there. Almost as if an invisible family occupies the house.

The sixth EVP also recorded in the living room was again on the unnerving side. The voice is that of a man who has an accent or colloquialism about the way he speaks. It says, *"Bury the sinner!"* When it says the word, *"sinner"*, it pronounces it *"sin-nah."* Of course, there is no way to prove who it is referring to, but once again, I was the only one in the house.

EVP number seven was recorded upstairs in the Pickman's former bedroom and sounds like a male child talking to someone. The voice clearly says, *"Bubba,"* then says, *"They are watching."* Then there are a couple of inaudible words, followed by what sounds like another child answering. But unfortunately, I can't understand what the second voice says.

The next EVP I found sounds like an older female. She says, *"All my promises!"* Not enough is said, to theorize what they might be talking about, but I get the impression, the woman is upset about something, The voice was recorded in the living room.

Several other voices as well as banging sounds and humming, were recorded during the night. Only one is clear enough to tell what was said. The voice says, "Boo," which is what one might expect a ghost in a haunted house to say.

I have recorded hundreds of EVP's over the years, and most sound benign in nature. But many of the voices I recorded at the Sallie House, sound negative if not threatening, which for me, offers additional evidence that psychic Peter James, was correct in his assessment, that a negative or demonic force was present, when the Pickman's lived in the house.

The question of why something so negative or possibly evil haunts the house at 508 North Second Street in Atchison, Kansas, will probably remain a mystery forever. The answer to this question and others may have been washed away with the historical records that were lost in the great flood. Did something so terrible take place at this location that a supernatural presence perceived it as an invitation to take up residence, waiting for the perfect person to torment and use to further its own sinister purpose?

Did a little girl named Sallie ever live in the house? If so, who was she? Or maybe a better question is, what was she? Tony Pickman saw the little girl on several occasions, but he also saw a much more ominous and hideous looking creature as well. Tony described to me what the creature looked like on several occasions, and what he described is what you would expect a demon to look like or see in your worst nightmare.

Over the years, I have come to know Tony and Deb very well, and I believe them to be honorable and honest people. One thing I am certain of, is Tony saw, and experienced, some very frightening things while living in the house. You can see it in his eyes when he talks about the experience. It's a look that tells me, he never wants to come face to face with it again.

Will paranormal investigators, like me, ever solve the mystery of the Sallie House? My personal belief, is no. I also believe that whatever is in the house, patiently waited for a person like Tony to come along, and probably won't show itself, until the right person comes along again.

If you decide to investigate the house, be careful, and don't let your guard down, because what resides there is real, lying-in wait for its next victim, to turn their life into a living nightmare. Don't let that victim be you.

Kentucky

SHANDIES
RESTAURANT

EIGHT

Located along the Tennessee and Ohio Rivers, in McCracken County, Kentucky, is the city of Paducah. The population, according to the U.S. Census of 2021, was 24,863 people. But what the Census Bureau failed to account for in their tabulation, are some of the residents from days gone by who still remain in this great city. Residents that is, of a more ghostly nature, who still roam the streets and buildings of this quaint river town. The former C.C. Cohen building which houses Shandies Restaurant, located in the heart of downtown Paducah, at 202 Broadway Street, is a place that seems to house a few of these spirit folk.

The building is believed to have been built somewhere around 1865. Over the years it has served various purposes, including a clothing and dry goods store. In 1914, the Paducah City Directory identified the occupants as the R.L. Peacher Liquor Dealers and the Rehkopf Distilling Company. The Cohen family owned the location from 1921 until 1980, when Stella Cohen Peine, the last resident of the Cohen family, died in the building. Many Paducah residents believe that she never left and still roams the structure.

This is what makes a great restaurant like Shandies so enticing to a paranormal adventurer like me. Not only do they have great food and drinks, but they also have a resident ghost that haunts the place. Most of the locals are aware of the haunting activity and how the ghost of Stella Cohen is believed to be responsible.

The Cohen's lived in the building directly above their businesses for many years. When Stella Cohen died, she wasn't found for several days because she lived alone and didn't receive many visitors. Her only companions were her two Doberman Pincher dogs. According to one source at the restaurant, who talked to an eyewitness, that observed the activities when authorities found her body, described the scene as pretty gruesome, because her dogs had not been fed for several days and had fed on her body. The witness described seeing one of the first responders rush out of the building as he became ill at the sight of what he had found.

No one I talked to is certain when the haunting activity began, but there are stories of how after the building exchanged hands in the mid-1990s, and the new owner took over, strange things started happening.

Shandies Restaurant Paducah, Kentucky

There are reports of workers who would lose tools, malfunctioning equipment, and the feeling that someone was watching them. Other stories tell of people passing by the building, who have witnessed an old woman looking out from the second story window. The witnesses say that the woman closely resembles Stella Cohen. Sources, I spoke to, not only believe that she watches over the building, but believe she interacts with workers and customers as well.

Based on a bit of paranormal circumstantial evidence I obtained during the investigation, I believe that not only does Stella haunt the building, but possibly her younger sister Goldie as well.

If you check out the Shandies Restaurant webpage, you will see that they offer a prime location, quality service, award winning food, hand-cut marinated steaks, and a wide range of spirits. I wonder if by a wide range of spirits, they are referring to Beer, Wine and Ghosts? Based on my experience during our investigation and from the eyewitness accounts provided to us by the restaurant manager, I would say, that the wide range of spirits description, is pretty accurate.

The legacy of the Cohen family in Paducah began with Stella's father Ike Cohen. Born in Poland, March 22, 1862, he came to the United States as a child, first living in Chicago, and then later moving to Louisville, Kentucky before finally ending up in Paducah. Prior to his death, Ike had been one of the oldest established businessmen in Paducah, having a business in the city for some forty-three years. He originally operated a store at 104 South Second Street, before moving to the location at second and Broadway which is now home to Shandies Restaurant. Ike Cohen passed away June 30th, 1931, at his home in the Terrell Apartments.

Stella Cohen's mother, Anna "Annie" Hynes Cohen, was known as a friend to many of the showboat owners along the Paducah riverfront. She also owned the Cohen Department Store at Second and Broadway. Born on January 1, 1870, in England, she moved to Paducah, KY with her parents in 1884. Her parents owned a pawnshop in Louisville, Kentucky before being enticed to Paducah by the large crowds, which the City Market area attracted. Seeing the possibilities for having a successful business, they decided to move and open a store in Paducah. In 1927 the business was moved to the location at Second and Broadway, where the business was being run by her son Carl at the time of her death.

Some accounts of deaths of Cohen family members that have been told over the years, seem to be inaccurate. I have read several articles related to the ghostly activity that takes place, which refer to the murder of Stella's husband, Bernard "Ben" Peine, in an alley behind his home. However, from newspaper accounts, it appears that Bernard Peine died in his home at Second and Broadway, at 9:30 a.m., on Christmas Eve morning, 1961, at the age of 89.

The obituary explains that Mr. Peine was a native of Indianola, Texas having moved to Paducah, from Houston, Texas only four years prior to his death. The obituary, further states that Bernard Peine belonged to the Masonic lodge and had been a member of the Masons for over fifty years. Survivors were listed as his wife Stella Cohen and several nieces and nephews.

Information I found on Stella indicates that she was born August 18, 1883 and died at her residence at Second and Broadway in Paducah, Kentucky on July 16, 1980. Some say that Stella was found dead in her upstairs apartment, but staff who work at Shandies, pointed out a location on the main floor of the restaurant near the front window, where they believe her body was found. So, I am a bit uncertain which location in the building is correct, but the source from the restaurant was fairly certain she was found downstairs.

Stella had two brothers. An older brother named Ruben, born on May 1, 1881, who died July 27, 1934, and younger brother Carl, who was born November 12, 1889, and died on October 6, 1968. In addition to her brothers, Stella had one sister, Goldie Cohen, born June 23, 1903, who passed away February 13, 1974. One source told me that Stella's brother, Carl, was attacked and robbed in an alley behind the building.

The source believed this might be where the misinformation about Ben Peine being murdered behind the building came from. As a result of injuries to Carl, the source said he was unable to live on his own, so Stella and Goldie cared for him until his death in 1968.

Based on information I found, Stella's husband, Bernard Peine, Goldie, Carl, and Stella Cohen herself, all died in the building at Second and Broadway. So, there are four deaths of well known, prominent town residents, who either lived, worked, or spent the final moments of their earthly lives, in this building.

I first read about the haunting at the C.C. Cohen building while doing research for possible locations to investigate in the state of Kentucky. Previously, I had conducted paranormal investigations in Arkansas, Illinois, Indiana, Iowa, Kansas, Missouri, and Tennessee. I wanted to add another state to the list of locations investigated, while staying fairly close to home, so Kentucky seemed like a good choice.

Reading about a location where witnesses have seen the spirit of a former owner peering out the window, objects being moved around and the feeling of being watched and followed sounded worthwhile of an investigation. After conducting additional research, I found out the owner was a woman, named Karla, who was listed as the owner of Shandies in one of the articles I read about the haunting of the Cohen building.

Karla was interviewed in the article, so I located her by doing a Facebook search, then sent a message to her. I explained in my message who I was, and that I am a paranormal investigator. I further explained of my interest in conducting an all-night investigation at the restaurant. It wasn't long, before I received a reply from Karla in which she provided a phone number where she could be reached. We played phone tag for a couple of days, but finally we were able to make contact and discuss doing the investigation, which she agreed to.

Paducah is a little more than four hours from my home in Taylorville, Illinois, so the plan was to arrive at our destination around 6:00 p.m., look around the scenic and historic riverfront, then have dinner at Shandies before setting up for the investigation.

In addition to being a restaurant, Shandies is also a popular bar due to its atmosphere and proximity to the riverfront. Since the investigation would take place on a Friday night, Karla told me they sometimes stay open later to accommodate the late-night crowd that may wander in. So, our investigation could start anywhere from 11:00 p.m. to 1:00 a.m.

Accompanying me on the trip would be investigator Jay who I picked up in nearby Springfield at 2:00 p.m., and investigator Chris, who I picked up at his house on the way to Paducah. Our drive was pleasant as it was a sunny afternoon with the temperature in the low seventies.

Just a few miles from our destination, we took Exit 37 off of Interstate 24 at the southernmost tip of Illinois and stopped off at Metropolis, Illinois. Metropolis is the official home of Superman and proudly honors its favorite son with a fifteen-foot bronze statue of America's superhero right in the middle of Superman Square. In 1972 Superman adopted Metropolis as his hometown, bringing new fame to the community. It wasn't kryptonite that forced us to stop off for a short refuge, but too much water, iced tea, and full bladders. After our brief pit stop, we were back on the road and a short time later, arrived at our destination.

Our early arrival gave us plenty of time to look around the Paducah riverfront. There were several city blocks of murals painted on the floodwalls of Paducah, which depict the rich history and heritage of Western Kentucky. Painted by muralist, Robert Dafford, the paintings seem to make the riverfront come to life, but a life and time of days gone by.

We took a leisurely stroll down the riverfront, to enjoy the murals on the floodwall and see Paducah's history in pictures. The murals were not the only beautiful spectacle on the riverfront as they overlook the confluence of the Ohio and Tennessee rivers. The perspective from above the rivers, offer a spectacular view of the waterways.

When I turned and looked toward second and Broadway, I spotted a large sign with vertical letters that spelled out C.C. Cohen. There, I thought to myself, is our destination for the night. Even though Paducah is a small city, the view in the sunlight seemed to offer a look of distinction to the buildings. Combined with the lively streets, and architecture it gave me a feeling that I had taken a step back into time, a feeling I would again have a short time later, when I walked into Shandies for the first time.

I arranged to meet Karla around 9:00 p.m., so we still had an almost three hour wait. When we walked in, the restaurant was busy, but a few tables were available, so a waitress seated us right away. A one-man band was playing near the front window, which added to the lively atmosphere of the restaurant. Behind us was a beautiful bar, but unfortunately, since we had an investigation to conduct, the only spirits we could have contact with on this night would be spirits of the dead, if we were to be so lucky.

We took our time eating and enjoyed the music, but it was getting close to 9:00 p.m., and I still hadn't seen Karla. So, I approached a waitress, who turned out to be the manager for the night. Her name was Toby, and at the time had been working at the restaurant for two and a half years. She told me that Karla would not be able to make it but had decided to allow us access to the entire restaurant for our investigation. This would include the dining area, bar, kitchen, basement, and the second floor, which had a large gathering and dancing area as well as another full bar.

The third floor of the building is an apartment, that was rented at the time, so we would not have access to the third floor. Toby explained, that when Stella Cohen lived in the building the third floor was only used for storage. So as far as she knew, Stella did not use the third floor at all.

There were still customers in the bar, and a few in the restaurant, so Toby couldn't lock the doors for the night, but said we could begin bringing our equipment in and set up as much as we could on the second floor. Then when the customers left, we could set up downstairs, which is what we did.

To get to the upstairs area, there is a door at the back of the restaurant. When exiting the door, there is a landing, and to the left are stairs to the second floor, and to the right is a door that leads outside to the front of Shandies. We headed upstairs and entered the door to the second-floor area. It was an area large enough for another complete restaurant. I'm only guessing, but I estimate the upstairs was one hundred feet long by sixty feet wide.

The second floor consisted of a beautiful bar. If facing the bar, directly to the left, is a large area with wooden tables and chairs. Across from the tables and chairs is a separate room, and what appeared to be a dance floor, which also had tables and chairs, that were pushed up against the wall. Heading past the dance area and walking toward the stairs, is a wooden railing that surrounds an opening in the floor. The opening was fifteen by fifteen feet. Looking over the railing, you can see the restaurant below.

Behind the upstairs bar, is a hallway, leading to the bathroom. At the opposite end of the hallway, is a small area used to hang coats. Just past this, is the back stairwell leading to the outside, which was locked.

A long folding table across from the upstairs bar, was used as our equipment staging area. We set up the DVR and monitor for the surveillance system on the table and stored our equipment bags underneath it.

Second Floor Bar

I placed one surveillance camera on a table near the windows facing the riverfront and pointed it toward the equipment staging area. A second camera was set up in the dance area, next to the wall. To do this, we had to move tables out of the center of the room and put them against the wall facing the riverfront. When we did this, the dance floor was completely clear. You will see the importance of this a bit later.

After moving the tables, we pointed the camera toward the second-floor entrance. I placed audio recorders, on an old fireplace mantel, a table in the dance area and one near the restroom. As we were setting up the equipment, Chris made a comment as to how warm it was, and that he was beginning to perspire. It was so warm; I thought about waiting until the customers left and moving our command center downstairs. You will see why I bring this up, momentarily.

It wasn't long before the customers started clearing out, so I went downstairs to ask Toby how soon it would be before we could begin setting up on the first floor. While talking to her,

I asked if she had any paranormal experiences while working at Shandies. She looked at me, smiled and said, *"Oh yes, many."* I asked if she would be willing to take us around to where her experiences happened and share her stories with us. She said she would be more than happy to.

There were a few customers still in the bar finishing up, as Toby led us to the kitchen area to begin the tour. I was caught off guard by her experiences because I had never heard of ghostly sightings in the building other than the Stella sighting in the upstairs window.

When we entered the kitchen, Toby explained how she often stays late at night and is alone while she finishes closing things down and making sure the equipment is turned off.

One night, as she was making her usual rounds, she turned the corner and walked into the kitchen. She was startled when she turned toward the sink, because there was a man standing there, with his back to her. At first, she thought someone had put a mannequin in the kitchen to play a joke on her, because the figure was solid, but was not moving. She stopped dead in her tracks when the man started walking away. *"It's definitely not a mannequin,"* she said to herself, *"but who is it, and what are they doing in the kitchen?"* She further explained that the figure walked toward the other side of the kitchen, then, after taking a few steps, vanished. *"The man simply took a step and disappeared,"* she said.

In the two and a half years Toby has worked at Shandies, she has seen the man three times. *"I always see him late at night after everyone else is gone,"* she explained. *"He always dresses and looks the same. He has sandy blonde colored hair, wears an ugly old orange t-shirt and blue jeans."* She has never seen his face, because the man is always facing away from her as he begins his short walk to nowhere.

The second time she saw him, she had a strange feeling she wasn't alone when she walked into the kitchen. Toby explained the uneasy feeling caused the hair to stand up on the back of her neck. When she turned the corner, and walked into the kitchen, he was standing just past the sink. Then, just like the first time she saw him, as soon as he walked across the kitchen, he vanished. The third time she saw him, was similar to the first two. He was standing in the same spot, took several steps, then disappeared.

Each time she saw him, Toby searched the restaurant, but never found anyone. As far as she knows, no one else has seen him or at least no one else will admit to it.

After the kitchen tour, Toby took us upstairs to the second floor, which is where several of the Cohen family, including Stella had lived. When we entered the upstairs, Toby noticed the air-conditioner was on. She knew it was not on earlier and wondered if we turned it on while setting up our equipment. I told her we had not and explained how hot it was earlier while setting up the equipment and now it was cooler. She laughed and explained that the air conditioner seems to mysteriously turn on by itself.

"When I first started working at the restaurant," she began. *"I would turn the air conditioner off, but when I returned later to check the upstairs, it would be on again, even though no one had been up there."*

Toby had a professional air-conditioning person she knows take a look at the system for her. The man explained that the unit has an older spin dial thermostat that could not turn on and off by itself, unless it was defective, which it didn't appear to be. So maybe earlier when we mentioned how hot the upstairs was, Stella or whoever haunts Shandies, decided to turn the air conditioning on for us.

Toby said that on several occasions in the last couple of years, she has detected an overwhelming scent of what she described as rose oil or rose glycerin. *"Usually when the odor is strong, unusual things happen, and Stella acts up,"* she said.

"One night I was upstairs checking to make sure everything was turned off, when out of the blue I began smelling the strong odor of rose oil. As soon as I smelled it, the air conditioner turned on by itself," Toby said. "It's spooky when you are alone, and a piece of equipment turns on and you know it shouldn't," she added.

On another night, before locking up to go home, she went upstairs to do a final spot check and walkthrough. "When I unlocked the door and walked into the upstairs, the lights and air conditioner were on. I checked the upstairs earlier in the evening, and everything was off. No one else had access to the upstairs because I was the only one who had a set of keys. To top it off, the door was locked when I came back upstairs," she said.

"Turning the lights off required walking across the room, which I didn't relish the thought of doing, knowing I was alone in a haunted building."

"Even though I was uncomfortable making the trek across the room to turn the lights and air conditioner off, it had been a long day and I wasn't in the mood for Stella's tricks. So, as I walked across the room, I said something out loud and a bit rude to Stella, that I probably shouldn't have. I didn't mean to be disrespectful, but wanted to get the point across, that enough is enough. I was tired and just wanted to go home. So, I told Stella, to stop the BS and leave things alone."

"After turning the lights and air-conditioning off again, I was locking the second-floor door, when a planter came flying down the steps from the third-floor landing and crashed nearby. I'm pretty sure the planter was a message from Stella to let me know she didn't appreciate my tone of voice, but I didn't stick around to find out," she said with a laugh.

When Toby got into her car that night and started to put the key in the ignition, a strong odor of rose oil filled her car. *"I believe Stella must have followed me to my car with the intent of coming home with me. So, in a stern voice, I told Stella she was not welcome or allowed to come home with me, and that she had to stay at the building, which is her home."* After making the statement to Stella, the rose smell dissipated.

Toby told of another similar incident that occurred on a different night. It was a night when she couldn't get the alarm system for the building to set. Toby explained that in order to set the alarm, there is a keypad and a four-number sequence to turn it on or off. *"I could hear the tone, for each keypad button I pressed, but each time, it sounded like additional numbers were being pressed, so the alarm wouldn't set."* Toby couldn't understand what was going on because this had never happened before.

"I had a bad feeling that something might be wrong, and that maybe Stella was trying to give me some type of warning that I needed to take a second look around. So that's exactly what I did." When Toby walked through the kitchen area, she found that one of the gas cooking burners for the grill was still on. *"I turned the grill off and thanked Stella for the heads up. With the age of the building, leaving a burner on all night could have been disastrous."* After turning the burner off and taking a final look around for the night, Toby walked over to the alarm system, pushed the appropriate buttons and the alarm immediately set exactly the way it should. With a sigh of relief, she thanked Stella for her help, and then headed home for the night.

As Toby was wrapping up our tour of the building, she explained that at times when she is upstairs, everything feels peaceful, but other times, she gets a feeling she shouldn't be up there, like she is intruding and not wanted. I know exactly what she is talking about, because I have had the same experience at a place called Ridge Cemetery in central Illinois.

Everything seems peaceful and quiet, then out of the blue, a feeling of dread or uneasiness will come over me. When this happens, I find myself looking over my shoulder, due to a feeling of being constantly watched and followed.

Toby explained that at times, the feeling is so strong, she will run from one side of the room to the other in order to complete the task at hand and get back downstairs.

"I haven't seen Stella in the two and a half years I have worked at Shandies, but I have heard footsteps coming from upstairs when no one else is in the building. It sounds like someone is walking on the upstairs floor and the footsteps are heavy enough, the wine glasses hanging above the bar downstairs, sway," she explained.

Toby told us a story about a former waitress who was working during the day shift. At some point, the waitress went into the women's restroom to freshen up a bit. While looking in the mirror, she took a photo of herself with her cell phone. As she took the photo, the lights turned off momentarily. When she checked the photo, she was shocked at what she saw.

"She came out of the bathroom and showed the photo to me," Toby said. *"In the photo you see the waitress, but standing behind her, is a dark silhouette of a person and no one else was in the bathroom with her. Shortly after showing the photo to me, her cell phone stopped working."*

Paducah is home to the National Quilting Museum, and throughout the year events are held downtown for quilting enthusiast. Toby told us of two separate, but similar instances, involving out of town quilters who stopped at Shandies to eat. On one occasion, Toby tried to seat a lady, who was in town for a quilting event, at a table located just to the right of the bar. The lady told her that she couldn't sit at the table because the spirit of a woman was already sitting there. The visitor explained that she is sensitive to spirits and can see the dead.

She further explained that the woman at the table watches over the building and enjoys watching people who come to the restaurant.

Not long after this, another woman, also in town for the quilting event, stopped in for dinner. Toby tried to seat the woman at the same table, but she also refused and requested another table. The woman explained she wanted a different table because the spirit of a woman was already seated at the table, and it wouldn't be right for her to intrude. Just like the previous lady, the woman was sensitive to spirits and able to see spirits of the dead. Toby laughed after telling the stories then added, *"What is it about ladies who quilt, being psychic?"*

The restaurant and bar had cleared out by the time Toby finished our tour of the building, and the remaining staff had gone home for the night. Now it was our turn, to see what goes on after the lights go out. Would Stella Cohen mind three strangers roaming around her home, and would she be up to any of her old tricks? We would soon find out.

The Investigation

When Toby and her staff left, we finished setting up our equipment downstairs. We dropped a video cable over the railing on the second floor and down to the first-floor bar area, where we set up a surveillance camera, which covered a good portion of the first-floor dining area. I also pointed a video camera at the table the psychic quilters claimed a spirit of an old woman sits. All of the cameras were infrared capable, which allows for recording in total darkness. Chris set up an additional camera in the kitchen in hopes of capturing the apparition of the man Toby has seen.

The first-floor area didn't give off any unusual feelings, but the second floor of the building seemed to have a different vibe to it. It's hard to describe the feeling other than the environment itself felt different. Nothing bad or threatening mind you, it was more the feeling you get when someone asks you to go into their home when they are gone, to make sure everything is ok, and even though you have permission to be there, you feel like you are invading their privacy.

The only area of the building I felt uneasy, was the area just outside the second-floor restroom. I'm not sure what caused the feeling, but when I was in this area, whether to use the bathroom or checking for temperature and EMF readings, it felt strange, like someone was hiding there. Because of the feeling, I placed an audio recorder near the bathroom. As it turned out, my hunch was right, because we recorded a voice near the bathroom, that didn't belong.

After setting up the equipment, we headed upstairs, to get the investigation underway. As we passed through the dance floor area, we noticed something. Earlier, I described how we had to re-arrange tables in order to make an unobstructed view for one of our video cameras. After moving the tables, the dance floor was clear of anything on the floor. But when we returned, one of the investigators, noticed a silver fork in the middle of the dance floor that wasn't there after moving the tables.

Investigator's Jay and Chris were certain the fork was not there before. Unfortunately, I was busy setting up the camera while they moved the tables, so I wasn't sure. One article I read about the Cohen building described how salt and peppershakers and silverware, would mysteriously move, and appear in places where they had not been placed. So was the fork in the middle of the floor, simply something we had overlooked, or was it placed there intentionally by an unseen phantom?

Since there were only three of us, in order to keep the investigation as a controlled setting, we stayed together the majority of the night. On one occasion Chris went downstairs and set at the bar, while we observed him on the upstairs monitor. Unfortunately, nothing happened, and no audio or video evidence was recorded.

No unusual activity occurred during the early part of the investigation, but halfway through the night, that would change. It happened while I was standing by the table we were using as our base of operation. As I was watching the video monitor, I witnessed one of the most unusual pieces of video evidence I have ever seen, and we recorded it.

The camera filming the incident was on the riverfront side of the upstairs, on a table near the windows. It was thirty feet away and pointed toward the bar and the equipment staging area. I was standing next to the table the monitor for the surveillance system was placed. Chris was behind and to my left, ten to twelve feet from the bar.

I was watching Jay on the monitor as he walked into camera range toward me. As he walked into the camera shot, I saw what looked like a small ball of light or what many investigators call an *orb*. At first glance I thought it was a piece of dust in front of the camera lens. Then I noticed it appeared to be following Jay. After watching the object for several moments, I called for the two investigators to take a look at what I was seeing. At first, it moved erratically, then slowed down and hovered. Then moving from left to right, it floated to where we were standing. It seemed to be checking us out, as we were watching it on the video monitor. We filmed the object for ten minutes and eight seconds, before it finally disappeared.

When I reviewed the video, at the one minute twelve second point into the recording, the object flies past my head then moves out of camera range momentarily. Then, it returns from the direction it originated, and not the direction it had exited the room, which didn't make sense. Momentarily, it hovers behind my head, before descending to my shoulders, then hovers behind the chair I sat in a few minutes earlier, then descends to my lower back and waist area.

Second Floor Shandies Restaurant.

As the object floated and hovered around us, Jay checked for environmental readings, using a Mel-Meter, a device that detects electromagnetic and temperature fluctuations. While doing this, Jay pointed his flashlight where the object should have been, based on what we were seeing on the video monitor, and nothing was there. On one occasion, it appeared to land on the Mel-Meter he was using, but when Chris pointed his flashlight at it, again nothing. There were no fluctuations in EMF or temperature.

The object wasn't visible by the naked eye. It was only visible with the use of the infrared video camera. So, it wasn't a bug, or we would have seen it when Jay and Chris aimed their flashlights at it. Plus, we didn't see any flying insects during the investigation.

At one point, the object moved behind the back of my chair, which confirms what we were seeing, wasn't simply dust or pollen in front of the camera lens, because the chair was between the object and the lens. Throughout the ten-minute event, an occasional speck of dust was seen drifting by the camera lens. The dust particles in no way reacted the same as the object did. I have reviewed thousands of hours of video from investigations over the years, with thousands of hours of dust, pollen, and moisture in them, as well as orbs caused by everything from insects to bats flying in cemeteries and buildings. The object recorded at Shandies, reacted nothing like anything I have witnessed before. It acted as though it was under intelligent control.

Since the investigation, I have shown the video to other seasoned paranormal investigators, who agree, that the object is not dust or pollen and appears to have an intelligence about it. So, what is it? Is it a spirit or an inter-dimensional entity? Is it connected to the paranormal activity in the building? Or is there a scientific explanation for what we recorded?

Shortly after recording the video, the investigative team and I were discussing what we saw. During the conversation, we recorded a loud whispery voice that was not one of the team members. The voice simply says, *"Wow,"* and was recorded by the recorder I placed near the upstairs bathroom, in the area that gave me an uneasy feeling. When it was recorded, we were discussing the orb and how it was only visible on the monitor and not with our naked eyes. So, was something reacting to our conversation because it, or they, realized we could see it?

Our investigation included two separate EVP sessions, where we asked questions, hoping to initiate a verbal response that either our audio recorders would capture, or we would physically hear the response. Unfortunately, we neither heard nor recorded anything during the sessions.

We also conducted two separate SB-7 Spirit Box sessions. The most productive session was upstairs near the dance floor, which produced four clear, what I believe were responses. I gave an explanation as to the origin of the SB-7

Box, and how the device works in Chapter Two of this book, and as I explained, based on how the box works, clear voices should not come through. But the voices we heard at Shandies, were perfectly clear.

During the box session, I asked the following question. *"Stella, was that you we saw as a ball of light or energy?"* There was no reply to this question, so I asked, *"Was it your sister Goldie?"* Three seconds after I asked the question, we heard and recorded a clear response say, *"Yes!"* I also asked, *"Goldie, did you like to play the piano?"* Within one point five seconds we heard and recorded another clear, *"Yes!"*

Many times, while conducting SB-7 sessions, you will hear voices and words spoken through the box without any prompting by asking questions. This was the case during the upstairs session, because at one point, the name, *"Stella,"* was clearly said by a female voice even though I hadn't asked a question.

As a private investigator, I was taught to evaluate evidence in as unbiased and logical manner as possible. When conducting paranormal investigations, I try to review and evaluate evidence in this manner as well, but how do you rationalize hearing a female voice coming through a radio device, when clear voices should not come through? Especially, hearing a voice saying *Stella,* which is no longer considered a common name. Not to mention, hearing the voice in a building reportedly haunted by a resident ghost with the same name. It is experiences like this, that keeps me coming back to see and experience more of what the paranormal has to offer.

Did the voice prove Stella Cohen was communicating with us? Of course not. But something seemed to understand what we were doing and knew we were interested in someone named Stella. The response did not appear to be simply a random voice, but something that was said so that we would hear it.

The more I use the SB-7 box, the more convinced I am that somehow, something, whether ghostly in nature, or from some invisible realm, can hear us, and is able to communicate with us. I don't believe however, a device is necessary for them to hear us but is necessary, for us, to hear them. The device seems to bridge the barrier between other realms of existence and ours, allowing us to hear sounds we normally would not be able to hear, due to sound frequencies, beyond our physical range of hearing.

Based on the responses we received through the box, it was possible, Goldie Cohen was speaking to us. So, I began asking questions of Goldie. The final response during the SB-7 session, came when I asked, *"Goldie, is your sister Stella here with you?"* Immediately after my question, a loud and clear male voice said, *"I don't know!* "Based on the box scanning the radio frequencies at the rate of 100ms per second, a statement like, *"I don't know,"* should not be possible.

If the voices that come through the box, are truly, spirits, inter-dimensional beings, or some type of life force from other realms, we unfortunately, have no way to know, if what is said, is meant to be helpful, playful, or spiteful. After hearing a fairly good number of responses come through the box since I have been using it, my best answer would be all of the above.

So, did the male voice which said, *"I don't know,"* say this, because it really didn't know the answer to my question? Did I get the *"yes"* answers when I asked questions about Goldie, because the answers were truly yes? Or were the responses just random communications that occasionally coincided with my questions?

One theory I have, is that in order to communicate with us, whoever these voices are, must wait for a frequency that allows them to access our realm. This would explain why correct or pertinent answers to questions we ask, sometimes come thirty seconds or more after the question is asked.

One final experience occurred, just after 3:00 a.m. It happened downstairs, while we were upstairs standing next to the table the video monitor was on. Suddenly, we heard a loud bang that startled all of us. It sounded like it came from the bar or kitchen area downstairs. My first thought was someone must have broken into the building. I took a quick glance at the monitor but didn't see anything on the screen. We ran down the stairs hoping to catch whoever was in the building. But after checking the restaurant, bar, and kitchen areas we found no one. We checked the bathrooms, and they were empty as well. Nothing had fallen over or off of the walls, nor did anything look out of place.

We captured the noise on our audio recorders, and it was deafening. It sounded like something heavy fell, or someone slammed a door shut. We never figured out what caused it but are certain that it came from inside the building.

The noise was the final event of the night, and the sun was coming up, so we began breaking down our equipment, packed up and headed back to Illinois.

Even though we didn't physically see a ghost or the spirit of Stella Cohen, the former C.C. Cohen building, more than lived up to its reputation. The evening started off with Toby telling stories about her personal experiences in the building. Her stories not only set the tone for the investigation but validated our first experience of the night, that of all things, involved the air-conditioning system turning on by itself.

The most unusual piece of evidence for the night, was the video of the strange, floating anomaly that maneuvered around us, as though it was under intelligent control. In all the years I have been investigating the unexplained, I have never witnessed anything like it. Can I declare it was the spirit of one of the Cohen family members or some other ethereal being? No, but I can't explain it either.

The SB-7 session proved fruitful as well. Radio frequencies

scanned, at a rate faster than a hummingbird can flap its wings, should not allow voices saying words and phrases to come through, yet they do. Without prompting, the name, *"Stella,"* was clearly said by a voice. The odds of the name Stella being recorded, in a building a woman of the same name is said to haunt, are astronomical.

Another occurrence we couldn't explain was the bang from downstairs. It sounded like a door slamming. When we heard the noise, I checked the video monitor, and saw no one. We immediately ran downstairs to investigate and if someone was in the building, we would have found them, but we didn't.

The combination of personal experiences, along with the video and audio evidence, made a believer out of me, that something unusual, and quite possibly supernatural, is taking place at the former C.C. Cohen building. So, if you are interested in ghosts and hauntings like I am, and are ever in Paducah, Kentucky, Shandies Restaurant is the perfect place to stop in for a visit. Their advertising pretty much sums it up. Prime location, quality service, award-winning food, hand-cut marinated steaks, and a wide range of spirits.

Missouri

ROCKCLIFFE MANSION

NINE

In 2007, I was fortunate to have the opportunity to investigate Hannibal Missouri's, historical and haunted Rockcliffe Mansion, with friends and paranormal colleagues, Dr. Gary Hawkins, and Paul Robinson. At the time, Paul worked for the local FOX television station in Columbia, Missouri. I had previously investigated with them at another well-known location in Hannibal, the Stillwell Murder House.

Paul was in the process of filming a documentary called Haunted Hannibal and had been utilizing Dr. Hawkins to assist him in the venture. Gary knew of my interest in paranormal investigating, so he was kind enough to invite me to assist them with the Stillwell Murder House also known as the LaBinnah Bistro and Rockcliffe Mansion investigations. So, I gladly accepted the opportunity to investigate with them.

Rockcliffe Mansion was built in 1900 by wealthy lumber baron, John Cruikshank. Cruikshank wanted a house he could showcase the finest woodwork and furnishings that money could buy. The mansion was built using the highest quality walnut, oak, and mahogany available at the time. The exterior of the building consisted of double brick construction. Today, the mansion still houses many of the original furnishings used by the Cruikshank's.

The family consisted of John, his wife, and four daughters. They lived in the mansion along with their butler until John's death in 1924. After his death, the mansion was vacant for over forty years. It was weeks away from being torn down, when a local group got together at the last minute and purchased the old mansion, restoring it back to its original form. Today, tours are conducted at Rockcliffe, and it is also a seasonal bed and breakfast. The mansion is enormous, spanning 13,300 square feet, including nine bedrooms and seven bathrooms.

Some believe the mansion is haunted by the spirits of John Cruikshank, his wife, four children, and their butler. The owner at the time of our investigation claimed he once saw an impression of a figure in the bed sheets on one of the beds. Many guests have smelled cigar smoke in a room in which Mark Twain once stayed. Twain, a friend of John Cruikshank, gave his last speech in Hannibal in 1902 and stood on the third step of the main staircase, as he addressed a crowd of three hundred invited guests. There are reports of local television crews who come to film at Rockcliffe, having camera batteries go dead or their cameras malfunction.

On the day of the investigation, Gary and I arrived at the mansion at 2:00 p.m., and Paul a short time later. The plan was for Paul to conduct interviews and videotape eyewitness accounts of people who experienced paranormal activity at the mansion. In addition, Paul had placed an ad on Craig's List, for three people to attend the investigation, who had an interest in ghosts and hauntings but had never been on a ghost hunt before. The reason for this, was so he could film their candid reactions to potential activity that may occur during our investigation. Over forty people applied for the opportunity to attend, and Paul selected three of them. They were due to arrive between 5:30 p.m. and 6:00 p.m.

While Paul was busy setting up for the interviews, Gary gave me a quick tour of the mansion. We were walking through the main floor of the building, when a young lady who works at Rockcliffe stopped us. She wanted to let us know that she was leaving, but would be back a little before 7:00 p.m. to set up decorations in the basement for a bachelorette party to be held from 8:00 p.m. until 10:00 p.m. The party was for a close friend of hers, and she stressed that they would keep the noise down, because she knew we were investigating.

The lady told us about an unusual experience she had only a few weeks before. She was working one evening and was sitting at a desk near the main entrance. *"It was raining outside, of course,"* she laughed. *"The doors were locked, and I was alone in the mansion. Suddenly, I heard footsteps directly above me."*

"I said to myself, you didn't hear that, trying to convince myself, that I only imagined hearing the noise. Moments later, I heard the footsteps again, and a few minutes after that I heard them for a third time. After the third time, I stood up and walked to the foot of the staircase and yelled upstairs. If you are trying to scare me you are not doing a very good job!" After confronting the noise, the footsteps stopped.

At 5:00 p.m., Gary took a walk around the grounds of the building, so I left him and accompanied Paul, who was filming daylight footage of the mansion. We were coming down the main staircase, from the second floor, when Paul saw a shadow to his left, in an area on the first floor, near the dining room. Due to the angle of the staircase, there was a limited view of the dining area from where we stood. Paul described what he saw as a shadow that completely blocked out the entire portion of wall where the wood wainscoting and the wallpaper met, at the entrance to the dining area. Trying to recreate what Paul saw, we backed up and repeated our path down the stairs and the shadow was not there.

At 6:00 p.m., a couple from St. Louis named Kimberly and Tony arrived, and Chuck, a gentleman from Hannibal, arrived shortly thereafter. The trio had responded to Paul's advertisement. Upon their arrival, we took them to the main dining room area, where Gary and Paul gave our new friends a brief rundown on what to expect during the evening, including how the investigation would be conducted. Gary, who is also a tour guide for haunted tours in Alton, Illinois, usually gives what he calls his *Ghost 101* speech to folks who have never been on a tour or paranormal investigation. His talk includes a rundown of theories as to what ghosts are, and the forms in which they appear. He further explained, they should be prepared to expect the unexpected, even if they were skeptical about the existence of ghosts.

With the exception of Gary, who stood at the head of the table with his back to the main living area, the rest of the group was seated at the table. On one side, with our backs to the main entranceway, were Kimberly and I. Kimberly's boyfriend, Tony, sat at the far end of the table, seated next to Paul. On the other side of the table, across from me, was Chuck.

In addition to his Ghost 101 speech, Gary explained our plans for dinner. Normally, after the mansion closes for the day, the owner locks all of the doors and sets the alarm system so no one can enter without being detected. In order for us to have access afterhours, the owner left one door unlocked for us to go in and out. We were told that if everyone left, we would have to lock up and would not be able to re-enter. So, in order for us to go to dinner, our plan was to wait for the employee, who would be returning at 7 o'clock to finish setting up for the bachelorette party. When she arrived, we would let her in, so we could leave to go eat, and when we returned, she would unlock the door and let us in.

Momentarily, you will see the importance of the lady returning, due to a strange event that took place and left our entire team dumbfounded.

At 6:30, as Gary was finishing his talk, I noticed Tony had a puzzled look on his face, sort of a frown. Finally, he said, *"You guys may think I'm crazy, but I keep seeing shadows through the doorway, moving across the living room floor."*

Interior Rockcliffe Mansion

A short time later, I noticed a similar expression of puzzlement on Chuck's face, just before he exclaimed, *"Tony, you're not crazy my friend, I keep seeing shadows moving across the wall in the living room myself!"* With the comments of the two, I started to get excited, because if folks were seeing things in the middle of the day, we might be in for an eventful night.

It was ten minutes before 7 o'clock and the young lady in charge of the bachelorette party had not returned. I suggested to the group, if they wanted to leave to go eat, I would stay behind and watch the place and they could bring my supper when they returned. Gary proposed we give her a few more minutes and if she did not return by 7 o'clock, they would do as I suggested.

It was shortly before 7 o'clock, and Kimberly, Tony, and I all turned, and looked toward the side door that the owner gave us access to. The door was locked from the inside, but we heard what sounded like someone unlocking the door, shutting it hard, then drag something across the hardwood floor. As soon as I heard the noise, I said to Gary, *"The girl's here, let's go eat,"* to which Gary eagerly agreed.

We arose from the table and walked into the main living area, then headed toward the door leading to the basement. Gary yelled downstairs to let the lady know we were leaving for dinner and that she would need to let us in when we returned, but no one answered. He yelled a second time, again with no reply.

Gary and I looked at each other, then proceeded down the basement steps. We looked around but no one was in the basement. We searched the entire mansion and discovered no one was there other than the six of us.

We started to open the door to see if she had gone outside to retrieve something from her car, but when Gary grabbed the doorknob to open it, it was still locked from the inside. Kimberly, Tony, and I reassured each other that we had heard, the door open, close hard and then heard something being dragged across the floor. So, if no one came in, what caused the strange sounds?

Since the young lady had not shown up yet, and it was 7 o'clock, we decided to implement our plan, and I would stay behind to keep an eye on the mansion while the group went to dinner.

As we gathered beneath the chandelier in the main foyer, discussing the dinner plans, we heard a metallic tapping sound. It sounded as though someone was nervously tapping their fingernails on the chandelier directly above us. This went on for several minutes, then stopped. We tried to come up with an explanation for the mysterious tapping but couldn't.

After the group left, I locked the door behind them and

grabbed my digital recorder and camera to do a bit of exploring, in hopes of capturing evidence while the group was gone.

All was quiet as I walked through the rooms of the main floor. Then, out of nowhere, I heard another tapping sound. It was a tap-tap-tap, that would start and stop, then start again. I couldn't figure out where it was coming from, other than it wasn't coming from the first floor. I headed up the main staircase to the second floor and walked through each room. Determining the sounds were not coming from the second floor, I continued my search on the third floor. Once again, I searched every room, trying to identify the source of the tapping, but found nothing.

One room on the third floor, gave me an odd feeling. It was the former ballroom, which had also been used as a playroom by the Cruikshank children. The walls were painted sky blue, and the woodwork trimmed in white. The restored wooden floor had a dull look to it like it was still being used. With every step I took, the floor creaked, just like in the old Bowery Boys movie, Ghost on the Loose. I felt like I was being watched.

I determined the tapping sound wasn't coming from the third floor, so the only possible location it could be coming from was, you guessed it, the basement.

This time, I used the staircase on the west side of the mansion. As I neared the first floor, the tapping sound started again. The dilemma I was now faced with, was whether I wanted to go down to the basement of a haunted mansion alone. I had seen plenty of horror movies and knew how that usually turned out. But, my investigative nature overtook my lack of better judgment, and I continued my trek to the basement crypt.

There were several rooms in the basement, along with a stage the owner used to host cabaret type shows and other functions. The tapping sound was coming from what I later determined to be a kitchen or food preparation area. I continued walking toward the noise and realized that it wasn't a ghost causing the tapping but was a hot water pipe used in the heating of the house. I was both relieved and disappointed that I wouldn't be confronting a ghost.

After my wild goose chase I headed back upstairs and camped out in the dining area. I sat where Tony had been seated earlier in hopes of catching a glimpse of the shadows he and Chuck had seen. My stakeout of the dining room was interrupted when the lady finally arrived to finish the decorations for the party. I asked her if she had arrived earlier and left, and she said no. I explained what we experienced earlier, and laughing, she said, *"That doesn't surprise me, you never know what the mansion has up its sleeve."*

During the hour and a half, the team was gone, nothing happened. The group returned shortly after 8:30, so it was time to get the investigation underway. Our plan was to set up infrared surveillance cameras and audio recorders throughout the mansion. Two rooms we set up cameras in, were rooms staff and guest had seen or heard things. One of the rooms on the first floor, was a favorite of Mrs. Cruikshank. As the story goes, she loved to play her grand piano in the room.

The other room of importance was the third-floor ballroom where the Cruikshank's hosted parties and was also used as the playroom for the children. Modern day guests of Rockcliffe have claimed to hear the sound of small footsteps walking and running throughout the mansion. Paul told me that during a previous investigation, he was standing on the second floor just below the ballroom when he heard the sound of small feet running across the floor. They tried to recreate the sound by having a team member run across the floor, but only when the person ran on his tiptoes, did it sound like what they had heard. He believes the phantom footsteps, were made by the ghost of the Cruikshank children.

Once our equipment was in place, we were ready to begin

the investigation. Gary provided a digital thermometer to Tony, and loaned his EMF detector to Kimberly, so they could monitor temperature and electromagnetic field readings. The purpose of the thermometer was to check for temperature fluctuations and the EMF detector was used to determine whether or not there were electromagnetic disturbances in the area. The main pitfall of an EMF detector is that it also picks up electromagnetic fields created by natural sources like wiring or electronic devices. So, investigators do an initial walkthrough of locations in order to identify natural magnetic fields and establish what the temperature of the location is.

We began the investigation in the room where Mrs. Cruikshank played her piano. Since there are two doorways for the room, we decided Gary would go in one door and the remainder of the team, would enter through the other. By entering the room in this manner, if a spirit was present and decided to leave due to our presence, it would have to pass by one of the groups and hopefully we would see it, or our equipment would detect it. So, Gary entered through the doorway on the right, while Paul, who was filming, and the other three members of the group entered through the doorway on the left. I followed Paul with my camera.

As Paul passed through the doorway, I heard Gary call out, *"It's cold over here!"* So, I decided to make my way around to the doorway that Gary entered from, in order to film him from a different angle than Paul. When I reviewed my video footage the next day, I found I had recorded a child's voice saying *"Momma."* The voice is heard as I am walking toward the doorway. It sounds like a female child looking for its mother.

While filming Gary, I noticed he extended his right hand forward, prior to announcing he found a cold spot. He then asked the three first-time ghost hunters to come forward, so they could experience the cold as well. When they felt the area, I could tell by the excitement in their voices, they were dumbfounded by the drop in temperature. But what would happen next, would leave them speechless.

While filming, Paul announced he saw an orb through his video camera, moving toward Gary. When he finished filming, we decided to take a short break to review the video footage. Paul asked me to film the reactions of our guest ghost hunters, while he replayed the footage of the orb he captured for them.

In the video, you can see what looks like a small ball of light floating toward Gary, before it reverses course and heads back in the direction it came from. The group was excited over what they were seeing, when Gary pointed out something else in the video. So, Paul rewound the footage and played it again. When he did, the reactions of the group were priceless. Chuck was in disbelief at what he was seeing, so much so, that he walked out of the room shaking his head.

(*This is what is seen in the video.*) First, the orb moves toward Gary, then reverses direction. My personal opinion of the orb is that it is some type of flying insect. A second or two after the orb reverses direction, and with Gary standing completely still, a shadowy silhouette of a man can be seen walking behind Gary, heading toward the doorway where I am standing. The silhouette walks in the opposite direction Gary is facing, then exits the room.

I was shocked as I watched the video. There was no source of light to cause the shadow. The only light was coming from outside through a window behind Gary. If the outside light had caused the shadow, it should have been in front of Gary, not behind him. Not to mention, someone would have to be behind Gary, and there wasn't. Everyone, with the exception of Gary and I, were standing next to, or behind Paul. I was standing just outside the doorway across from Paul and to Gary's left and I was standing completely still. So, everyone and all sources of light were accounted for, and there was no logical explanation for the shadow man. It was as though Gary's own shadow walked away from him without Gary moving.

The three guest ghost hunters, two of which were skeptical

of ghosts and hauntings when they arrived, were puzzled by what they were seeing. They tried to come up with a logical explanation for the shadow, but try as they may, they couldn't. They knew everyone was accounted for and the only other person in the mansion was the girl in the basement.

I could tell Chuck was shook up by what he saw in the video. He was shook up because what he was seeing didn't have a rational explanation and couldn't be explained with logic, which is what investigating and trying to solve the mysteries of the paranormal is all about. After the excitement of the shadow died down, we headed to the second floor, but all was quiet. So, we moved to the third-floor ballroom to continue the investigation.

The ballroom is basically an empty room with a few items stored in it. On one side of the room there were several mannequins dressed in period clothing and a small doll propped up near the mannequins. The items gave the room the feeling that children still occupied it. The restored wooden floor had a dull look to it, as though it was still being used as a playroom by the Cruikshank children.

Paul and I were using handheld video cameras and one of Gary's infrared surveillance cameras had been filming the entire evening. A digital voice recorder was on a small end table in the room, in hopes of capturing disembodied voices. The group spread out, sitting on the floor on different sides of the room and leaning against the walls.

After being in the room for fifteen minutes or so, I thought I heard a child murmuring. I wasn't sure, so I didn't say anything, but Paul did, because he asked, *"Did you hear that?"*

To which I replied, *"I did."*

"It sounded like murmuring," Paul continued.

"Like a child?" I questioned.

"Yes like a child," Paul said, confirming what I heard.

Upon reviewing video footage, the murmuring can be heard just before Paul says, *"Did you hear that?"* The murmuring was recorded three separate times by my handheld video camera. Each time it is heard, it is verbally acknowledged by a member of the group.

After Paul and I heard the murmuring, Gary decided to walk around the room. When he passed to my right, he said he felt something brush up against him and the air seemed colder where he was standing. Neither Paul nor I, who were filming Gary, could get our video cameras to focus on him. It was like our cameras were trying to focus on something invisible between Gary and us, causing his image to blur. Several minutes passed and Gary announced the cold air was gone. On cue, both cameras were able to focus again.

Soon after, I thought I saw a shadow move across the room, so I asked Gary to check it out for me. When he got to the spot, he said, *"You saw something, it's extremely cold here."* As Gary was standing in the spot, he placed his hands in his pockets. A few seconds later, I saw the shadow of an arm and hand move up and down. The shadow was cast on the wall to Gary's right, and his hands were still in his pockets.

Immediately I said, *"Gary, did you move your hand?"* "No," he replied.

At the same time, Paul asked, *"Did you hear that?"*

When I replayed my video footage, I had captured the shadow of an arm and hand moving up and down on the wall behind Gary. In the video, as Gary moves slightly forward, the wall behind him is lit up by the infrared beam from my camera. Suddenly, the lighted area, disappears and a shadow appears behind Gary. What makes the shadow so interesting, is Gary is standing perfectly still as the shadow blocks out the light behind him. Upon further review of the video footage, I noticed a murmur can be heard immediately before Paul asked, *"Did you hear that?"*

Many times, EVPs are recorded but are not physically heard. This time however, we heard the sounds, and recorded them. During evidence review a few days later, I found that in addition to the murmurs, several sounds were recorded when no one was in the room. The recording sounds like someone holding a mop by its handle, then lets go, allowing the handle to fall and hit the wooden floor. It was recorded on two occasions when no one was in the room.

The final area of the mansion we investigated, was the basement. Even though it was not as exciting as I had hoped for, I did have one experience while down there. It occurred while Chuck and I were standing near the stairs leading to the first floor. While standing there, we heard heavy footsteps followed by the sound of someone running across the floor above us. The entire group was in the basement, so we are positive it wasn't a member of the investigative team. After hearing the footsteps, Chuck and I ran upstairs to the first floor, but no one was there.

At 2:00 a.m., we decided to call it a night, said our goodbyes to Kimberly, Tony, and Chuck, then started packing up our gear. It was after Paul, Gary, and I finished packing up the rest of our equipment that I would have one last unusual experience at Rockcliffe.

I decided to use the first-floor bathroom just off the kitchen, before making the two-hour trip back to my home in Taylorville. It was dark in the bathroom, and I couldn't find the light switch. So, I returned to the kitchen were my equipment was stored and retrieved a flashlight, then headed back to the bathroom.

Entering the bathroom, I pressed the button to turn the flashlight on. When I did, the bulb made a popping sound, followed by a flash of light. Something caused the bulb in my flashlight to blow, cracking the glass and leaving a burnt mark on the lens. The flashlight was a few months old, so the bulb was new. I have had batteries go dead in flashlights, but never in my life have I had a bulb explode like that. Later I found out, that the bathroom I was using, was John Cruikshank's personal bathroom, and he never let anyone else use it. So, was the flashlight exploding paranormal or coincidence? Well, I have never had a flashlight powered by double A batteries explode before, or since for that matter. With that being said, I leave it up to you the reader to decide.

Summary

While investigating Rockcliffe Mansion, all of the classic TV movies about ghosts and haunted houses kept flashing through my mind. Because if I were making a movie about a haunted house, this would be the perfect place. With its rickety wooden floors that creak with every step, phantom footsteps, mysterious tapping on chandeliers, shadows that move about and disembodied voices recorded. The only thing missing is a secret passage that opens up by pulling out a book from the bookcase.

I don't have psychic abilities, but all throughout the twelve-and one-half hours that I spent in Rockcliffe Mansion, I had the feeling that the Cruikshank family is still living there.

Several times throughout the night, I explored the mansion alone, and felt as though someone was watching my every move.

Is Rockcliffe Mansion haunted, you ask? Well, let's examine the evidence.

The first piece of evidence was the eyewitness account of the young lady who works at the mansion. If you recall, she described an experience of hearing footsteps coming from the floor above her, while working late one night. Our investigative team also had several personal experiences, which began early on, with Paul, Tony, and Chuck, seeing shadows moving about the mansion.

Several members of the team, including myself, clearly heard the sound of a door being unlocked, opened, and what sounded like a heavy object being dragged across the wood floor. We thought it was the young lady returning to set up for the bachelorette party. However, upon investigating, we found the door still locked and no one in the mansion.

A forth piece of evidence took place on the third floor in the ballroom. Several times, Paul and I heard murmuring that sounded like a child's voice. On one occasion, Paul asked for whoever made the sound, to make it again. Within seconds we again heard the murmuring, as though it was listening and was trying to communicate with us.

The fifth piece of evidence occurred while we were in the basement and Chuck, and I heard someone running across the first floor directly above us. But when we checked, no one was there.

While on the third floor in the ballroom, our cameras captured the shadow of a hand and arm that moved behind Gary. But the most compelling piece of evidence captured on film was of a shadow behind Gary that walks out of the room. It was unbelievable. Everyone in the mansion was accounted for when it was recorded. So, none of the investigative team were responsible for the shadowy figure of a man.

The final experience of the night was my experience with the exploding flashlight in John Cruikshank's personal bathroom. Whether it was proof of paranormal activity or not remains to be seen, but how many times in your life have you switched on a flashlight, and it exploded? My guess is your answer is never.

So, is Rockcliffe Mansion haunted? Well, my answer is, "Yes!" There are simply too many credible stories and eyewitness accounts to go along with what I personally experienced to answer otherwise.

KEMPER MILITARY SCHOOL

TEN

Located between St. Louis and Kansas City is an interesting place, both rich in history and haunting activity, Kemper Military School, in Booneville, Missouri. The institution, originally known as the Boonville Boarding School, was built in 1845 by Frederick T. Kemper and became a co-ed institute in 1862, when it was renamed Kemper Military School. At one time, Kemper was the oldest boy's school west of the Mississippi River, until it officially closed in 2002. Its most famous alumni is Will Rogers, who attended the school in the 1890s. Rogers went on to gain worldwide fame as an actor, humorist, political commentator, and performer until his untimely death in a plane crash in 1935.

Kemper was the original choice for the location of several films, including National Lampoon's Animal House and Taps, but the school turned down both offers. It has been used as the setting for several other movies, including Combat Academy, a very low-quality takeoff on Police Academy, and Child's Play III. During the filming of Child's Play III, some cadets and instructors served as extras. In September and October 2007, Kemper's abandoned campus was used for location shots for the movie, Saving Grace, which is about a little girl's trip back to Boonville in the summer of 1951, the year of the great Missouri River flood. Many downtown Boonville buildings were used for filming, with Kemper the setting for an asylum. The movie, released in 2008, was directed by Connie Stevens and starred Penelope Ann Miller and Tatum O'Neal. My first investigation at Kemper took place in September of 2007. We wanted to do a follow up investigation but were delayed until December of that year, due to the filming of Saving Grace.

I became familiar with the school when paranormal colleagues Paul Robinson and Gary Hawkins asked me to help film a paranormal documentary about the haunting at Kemper.

Over the years, many have reported seeing the apparition of a female cadet, sometimes jogging, and sometimes walking near an outdoor track, vanishing when she nears the location where she was killed. According to accounts, the cadet had broken up with her boyfriend, but the boy talked her into going for a walk with him. During the walk, he raped and killed her near a bridge located on campus, not far from the jogging track.

D Barracks is reportedly the most haunted building on campus, with stories told about the fourth floor, in which a figure is seen standing in the window at night. For some reason, the fourth floor was closed to students. When I asked a former cadet the reason why, he told me because no one could stay up there. He said there was something about the floor that made visitors feel uncomfortable and even scared. Others claim to hear footsteps in C Barracks. Several years ago, while the barracks was being refurbished, construction workers reported hearing phantom footsteps. When they investigated, no footprints were found even though there was sawdust and dirt on the floor from the construction.

The team for the 2007 investigation consisted of Gary, Paul, and I, along with a cameraman and sound man from a local Fox TV station from nearby Columbia, Missouri. Paul was working for the FOX station at the time and asked the pair to join us, to add additional camera and sound support. I don't remember the soundman's name, but the cameraman's name was Eric. I remember Eric because he was very skeptical of ghosts and hauntings when he arrived but had a different outlook when he left. A writer named John, from *Inside*

Columbia Magazine, and the host of an internet-based paranormal radio show joined us for the early part of the investigation.

At the time the property was owned by the City of Booneville, so in order to gain access to the property, a lady from the city met us and unlocked several buildings for us, including "D" Barracks and the administration building. She gave us a general tour of the campus and told stories related to the hauntings. She told us that a paranormal group from Kansas City, Missouri had attempted to investigate the building a few weeks before us, but when the group went into Barracks D, several of their team members became ill and had to leave, so they called off their investigation.

When we entered the building there was an odd, heavy feeling that took your breath away. It was the feeling you get after running, and you feel winded from the run. Immediately upon entering the building, three team members spoke up, asking if anyone felt a heaviness in the air?" It was pretty uncanny to have three people bring up the same thing, at the same time. No one became ill, so at least we had passed the first test for the night.

After our tour of the campus and buildings, it was time to set up for the investigation. While the rest of the group went outside to gather up their equipment, I decided to stay inside and take a few photos in the kitchen of Barracks D. So, I was alone in the building.

Three to four seconds after taking a flash photo, another flash emanated from the back of the kitchen. It was like my flash had gone off again, but it hadn't. The flash came from across the room, so I called out and asked if anyone was there, but no one replied. *"Is anyone there,"* I called out a second time, again with no response. When I walked to the back of the kitchen, no one was there. I then headed outside and sure enough, everyone was accounted for. Explaining to the group what happened, they assured me they had been outside and hadn't taken any photos. I have no explanation for what caused the flash, because the kitchen is an interior room, with no windows, so the flash could not have come from the outside. Plus, the electricity was turned off in the building, so the flash could not have come from faulty lighting.

With one unusual incident under my belt, I was ready to get the investigation underway. Once inside, we did a sweep of the first floor of D Barracks together. Again, we found a spot in the building where the air felt very heavy and took our breaths away. During our trek through the building, we heard what sounded like moaning, but couldn't determine where it was coming from. The sound guy was using a parabolic microphone and wearing a headset and heard it loud and clear. Just outside the old mess hall, we heard a loud hollow banging sound, as if someone was banging on a drum or tom-tom! When we walked into the hall, the banging stopped. The banging was heard throughout the night, but we could never find the source. Later that night, when a former cadet of the school unexpectedly showed up, we told him about the banging and other noises we heard. The man had an explanation for everything we told him. Later in the chapter, I will tell you what he said.

After checking the mess hall, and not being able to determine where the banging was coming from, we decided to split into groups in order to cover the building faster. Eric and I would check out the basement area, while Gary, Paul, and the rest of the group would investigate the second floor.

The basement was huge, with one long corridor going completely around the building, with many rooms branching off of it. The lack of electricity added to the creep factor of the basement. Every doorway, nook, and cranny we walked past, gave the feeling that something was lurking in the shadows!

Eric and I walked through the corridor, filming, and using the LCD screens of our video cameras to find our way around. Each and every doorway we passed, caused an overwhelming feeling that someone was there and was going to jump out at us. I had this feeling every time I was in the basement that night.

At one point, I heard what sounded like someone groaning or clearing his or her throat. Since the sound was coming from behind me, I assumed it was Eric. A few second after hearing the sound, Eric said, *"Larry, did you hear that noise?"*

"Do you mean what sounded like someone clearing their throat?" I asked

"Yeah," Eric replied.

"I thought that was you," I said.

"No, it wasn't me," Eric responded.

"Well, if you didn't make the sound, and it wasn't me, then that means whoever made the sound is between you and me Eric!"

I can't repeat what he said, but he was startled and starting to believe that maybe there was something to this ghost stuff after all!

The groaning sound was the same sound we heard earlier on the first floor and picked up by the soundman's parabolic microphone. The odd and unfortunate thing from an evidence standpoint is, even though we all heard the groaning sounds, none of us recorded them, including the sound guy who had commercial quality recording equipment. Equally as strange, when we returned to Kemper in December of that same year, we didn't hear the groaning, but recorded it, which doesn't make sense.

Later in the evening, Paul and I investigated the third and fourth floors. The third floor was uneventful, so we headed to the fourth. We tried to enter the fourth floor through a stairwell door, but it was locked. Not only was the door locked, it was double locked by a heavy padlock and a steel deadbolt. We thought it was unusual for a door to an empty section of the building to be heavily secured in this manner

Since the door was locked, we made our way back to the third floor then headed to the stairwell on the opposite end of the building. This time we were in luck because the locks had been removed from the door.

When we entered the fourth floor, there didn't seem to be anything special or different to distinguish it from the others. There were just empty rooms.

One odd thing, however, was the temperature. The average temperature in the building was about 80 degrees and being on the top floor of the building, you would expect the temperature to be warmer than the other floors, but it wasn't. It was quite comfortable.

I made a comment to Paul that I was surprised at how cool it was. As Paul was agreeing with me about the cool temperature, I noticed sweat starting to roll down his forehead and the temperature became noticeably warmer. So, one moment it was cool and comfortable and the next, we were burning up!

Walking a few feet further, we noticed the temperature was cooling down again. Rather than walking into a cold spot which I have experienced many times on paranormal investigations, it seemed like we had walked into a hot spot. Or did we?

Could the hot spot actually have been the normal temperature of the forth-floor and the rest of the floor unusually cool for some reason? We couldn't figure out why there was such a fluctuation in the temperature, so we continued on.

Staircase 4ᵗʰ Floor

After investigating the fourth floor, Paul and I headed back to the second floor and joined Gary, Eric, and the sound man. By this time, the reporter and the radio personality had left for the night.

We were telling Gary about the extreme temperature fluctuation on the fourth floor, when we were interrupted by a loud tapping noise. It was *a "tap, tap, tap"* sound, and sounded like someone was walking down the hallway. We searched the second floor and couldn't find the source of the tapping but would hear it several more times during the night.

Next we headed back to the basement since Paul had not investigated there yet. Gary decided to take a break outside to get some fresh air, so the rest of the group headed downstairs without him.

We were in the basement for twenty minutes or so, when Paul's cell phone rang. It was Gary calling from the parking lot. He told us that a guy claiming to be a former cadet had arrived and was telling him about some of the experiences he had while attending the school. Gary thought Paul may want to film an interview with him, which is exactly what he did.

The cadet's name was Pierre. Pierre had attended the school in the 1970s while in Jr. High and High School. He was very friendly, and when he found out what we were doing at the school at night, he really opened up. He asked if we had experienced anything unusual, so Paul told him about the sounds we were hearing, such as the moaning, tapping, and banging sounds in D Barracks.

Pierre smiled and said, *"I think I might be able to explain all of the sounds you are hearing."*

He told us the groaning was caused by the spirits of the victims of a double homicide and a murder-suicide that happened in the kitchen and Mess Hall of D Barracks. *"It all started when a cadet was dating one of the kitchen helpers,"* he said. *"Theirs was a rocky relationship. One day, the boyfriend came in and shot his girlfriend point blank, killing her. He then turned the gun on himself. I believe it is their spirits haunting the building,"* he explained.

Next he interpreted the tapping sounds that we were hearing. Pierre said when he was a cadet, the officers would walk around the barracks at night, to make sure all lights were out, and everyone was in bed. Only the officers were allowed to wear metal taps on their shoes. So, during bed check, the cadets would hear the officers making their nightly rounds.

"As they walked around, you could hear the sound of the taps on their shoes echoing down the hall," Pierre explained. *"You didn't want to hear the sound of the tapping stop in front of your door, because if they did, something was wrong, and you were in trouble."*

We asked Pierre if he knew what the hollow banging sound

was that we heard. *"I sure do,"* he proclaimed. *"The officer of the day had a wooden desk that sat at the front of the Mess Hall. We only had a short time to eat, and at the end of each meal, the officer of the day read the daily announcements. To signal it was time for the announcements to be read, he would bang a small metal rod against the side of the desk. Once the officer banged the metal rod against the desk, the cadets immediately stopped eating and laid* their *utensils on the table. If they didn't, they would receive demerits.*

When Pierre finished his story, he asked if we had been to the fourth floor. Paul and I explained we had just been up there and told him about our experience with the temperature fluctuation. *"That doesn't surprise me,"* he said. *"When I was a cadet, the fourth floor was off limits and was kept locked so no one could access it."* When we asked him why it was off limits, he said the floor gave off a bad vibe and no one liked being up there, so the school closed it off.

"Even though it was locked and off limits, if you were brave enough to go up there, the cadets had a way to get to the fourth floor. I know this because a friend of mine had a terrifying experience up there."

Pierre explained that his friend was a tough guy and a member of the school's football team. *"He didn't fear anyone or anything."*

"One day, someone dared him to sneak up to the fourth floor and spend the night. So, he took the bet. That night, he snuck out of his dorm room and went up to the fourth floor."

Pierre said his friend wasn't up there more than a couple of minutes, when he came flying down the stairs like he had been tossed. *"He was trembling and nearly hysterical. I asked him what happened, and he told me he didn't want to talk about it. He said he was never going back to the fourth floor again. Finally, I was able to calm him down and convince him to tell me what happened. He said he was headed down the dark* *corridor when he heard someone behind him with what sounded like they had taps on their shoes. Before he could turn around, he heard a loud voice say, "**What are you doing on my floor?**" Assuming it was one of the officers of the day, he turned around. When he did, what he saw was not an officer, nor was it a human. He said he wasn't sure what the hell it was, but he didn't stick around to find out."* Pierre said he had never seen his friend so scared before or after his experience on the fourth floor. *"He would never talk about the experience again and he never went back to the fourth floor."* Pierre said shaking his head.

The various buildings had an odd feeling about them for most of our investigation, especially Barracks D. It was like we were not welcome. But after Pierre arrived, the feeling went away. I wondered if the feeling changed because Pierre was an ex-cadet, and belonged there, while we were intruders having never attended the school.

The only other interesting thing that happened that night, happened while we were investigating the administrative building. Everyone was in the building, except Gary. His back was giving him problems, so he went outside and sat on a bench to see if the pain would subside. Suddenly he came rushing in the building. *"You'll never believe what I just saw,"* he proclaimed.

Gary went on to explain that while sitting on the bench, he saw someone walking across the courtyard. He watched them as they got closer and noticed they were dressed in a cadet's uniform. Besides Pierre, no one else was on the campus that we knew of, and the school closed in 2002, so no one should be dressed as a cadet. *"Whoever it was went behind a building, and I never saw them again,"* Gary explained.

I'm not sure what Gary saw, but he saw something. He was not one to jump to conclusions, always searching for a logical explanation to debunk encounters during investigations. We all agreed that it was highly unlikely someone would be roaming around a closed military campus in a cadet's uniform, at 3:00 a.m.

As daylight approached, we began breaking down our equipment to get ready to make the four-hour trip home. We had several unusual experiences during the night, including the tapping, banging, moaning, and groaning sounds, temperature spikes, and Gary seeing the apparition. Unfortunately, no audio or video evidence was captured during the September investigation.

In December 2007, we returned to Kemper. This trip was not as pleasant as the first, and as a matter of fact, it was quite treacherous. When I left my home in central Illinois, it was forty degrees and raining, but by the time I met up with Gary in Alton, Illinois, the temperature had dropped to thirty-two degrees with sleet and freezing rain. When we arrived at Kemper, the temperature was down to twenty-three degrees and the freezing rain continued.

At the school, we met up with Paul Robinson and a couple of paranormal investigators from St. Louis, Missouri who specialized in high-tech audio. The contact lady from the City of Booneville met us at the abandoned school and gave us the key to get in.

The parking lot was like a frozen tundra. We had to find a convenience store to purchase a large bag of rock salt, to spread on the sidewalk and parking area to melt the ice, just so that we could walk without falling down. After spreading the salt our footing was more stable, so we began unloading the equipment. Detecting cold spots would be tough because it was only twenty-nine degrees inside the building.

Paul and the two-team members from St. Louis decided to set up our base for the investigation in the old mess hall of the barracks. While they were doing this, Gary and I set up surveillance cameras in the kitchen area and a stairwell that led to the second floor. The kitchen was in a separate room from the mess hall, and where we were, was seventy-five to one-hundred feet from where the other team members were setting up base camp.

As Gary and I were arranging the cameras in the kitchen, we heard a woman's voice coming from the mess hall. She was talking loudly and laughing.

I said to Gary, *"Who's the woman Paul and the guys are talking to? Did the lady from the city come back?"*

"I don't know," replied Gary. *"But I wonder what's so funny. Let's finish setting up this last camera and go see who is here. We need to tell them to tone it down a bit, so our recording equipment doesn't pick up their conversations."*

We finished setting up the cameras then headed to the mess hall to see who the lady was. When we walked into the hall, Paul and the two investigators were setting up equipment on a table, but no one else was in the room. I said to Paul, *"Did the lady from the city come back?"*

"No," he replied, *"why?"*

"Well, who was the girl you guys were talking to and what was so funny?" Gary questioned.

"No one else is here, but the three of us," Paul replied. *"Why do you think there was a girl here,"* he added.

We explained how Gary and I clearly heard a conversation and laughter of a woman that sounded like it was coming from the mess hall. *"Her voice was loud, and she seemed to be having fun,"* I said. Paul assured us that no one else was there, and they had not heard the voice or laughter of a woman. Unfortunately, when Gary and I heard the voice, our equipment was not yet recording as we were still setting up. We wondered if we heard the voice of the female who was murdered in the kitchen at the hands of her former boyfriend.

Because, who else would have reason to haunt the kitchen area of the building, and why? The experience was definitely weird. It was one thing to hear the voice and laughter, but quite another to have a witness hear the same thing!

Unfortunately, the voice and laughter was the only experience we had during the December 2007 investigation, as the rest of the night turned out to be mundane.

When I returned home and reviewed the evidence from the investigation, I discovered I recorded the moaning and groaning sounds. It was the same moaning and groaning we heard during the September investigation but didn't record. This time we didn't hear the moaning and groaning but recorded it. I guess all you can do is chalk up experiences like this, as another mystery of the supernatural.

The two investigations at Kemper Military School were fruitful and enlightening. Fruitful in that we had several personal experiences, including, hearing the moaning, tapping sounds, and banging during the September investigation. Then Gary and I hearing the voice of a woman talking and laughing in December. Both of us hearing it, meant we were not imagining what we heard.

Enlightening in that former cadet Pierre was able to give us plausible explanations for the unexplained noises we heard in September. If he is right, then what we heard was of supernatural origin. I always try to find a natural or logical explanation for things I experience, but how do you rationalize a voice or laughter that comes out of thin air!

If what we have been taught about the existence of Heaven and Hell is true, and I for one believe they exist. Then the possibility that other realms and dimensions exist is high. If they do exist, then so does the possibility of interaction with the things that dwell there. If our experiences at Kemper are any indication of the type of strangeness that these other realms have to offer, then you better buckle in, because it's going to be a heck of a ride.

MORSE MILL HOTEL

ELEVEN

The Morse Mill Hotel, or the Blue Lady, as current owner Patrick Sheehan calls it, is located just west of St. Louis near the small town of Hillsboro, Missouri. Originally built in 1816 as a one-room house, it was later expanded to its current size of 5,300 square feet, but there is some confusion as to when this expansion took place. Some say it occurred in the 1830s, while others say it took place in 1847.

John Morse came to Jefferson County in 1847 and built a commercial gristmill on the Big River, using slave labor to quarry the stones for the building. He also built a home in the town, which was named after his first commercial venture, Morse Mill. Morse who would go on to be a state politician, owned several general stores, a contracting company, and the hotel. After his death, his home was used as a stagecoach stop and became known as the Riverside Hotel. Eighteen sleeping rooms were added onto the home to accommodate the guests.

Morse, a premier bridge builder and engineer originally used the Morse Mill as his family residence. Since then, it has been used as a hospital for Confederate prisoners of war, a hotel, a brothel, a speakeasy, a United States post office, and a half-way house. It is also rumored to have been a stop on the Underground Railroad.

Morse Mill was also home to the first known female serial killer in America, Bertha Gifford. Gifford was born Bertha Alice Williams in 1876 and died in 1952, in a mental institution. She lived in Missouri where she acquired a reputation as an angel of mercy by showing up at the homes of sick friends and family, many of whom subsequently died. Their deaths began to make people suspicious, and Gifford was eventually arrested for murder. She was tried and found not guilty due to an insanity plea and spent the rest of her life in a mental hospital. Gifford is believed to have murdered as many as twenty-three people and possibly more.

A headstone with the name Bertha Gifford is located in a small cemetery down the road from the hotel, but according to some, she is not actually buried there.

Many famous people have walked the halls of the Morse Mill Hotel, including Al Capone, Charles Lindbergh, Charlie Chaplin, Clara Bow, and Frank Dalton, who claimed to be Jesse James, is also alleged to have stayed there, although there is no evidence any of the James gang stayed at the hotel.

I first heard of the Morse Mill Hotel while doing an internet search for haunted locations to investigate. I found an article about a documentary called the Morse Mill Project that was filmed in November of 2008. The article described how, during the filming, investigators reported seeing the shadow of a large man. They told of cameras levitating off the floor and rotating 360 degrees by themselves. The investigators claimed while upstairs, they heard a loud metallic sound, and when they returned downstairs to investigate the noise, they found an iron fireplace poker twisted in a u-shape. One filmmaker claimed she was scratched through her clothes by an unseen force, and another said they were scratched on the neck by three invisible fingernails.

An article in Haunted Times Magazine indicated that when the Morse Mill was a homeless shelter, residents saw a nine-foot-tall black shadow figure, while others saw faces in mirrors. Other guests have told stories of shadow people walking about the property, and down the road that passes by the hotel. The stories were intriguing, but sounded too good to be true, so I decided to see for myself.

I emailed a psychic from Iowa mentioned in the Morse Mill Project article and asked if she could provide a phone number for the owner of the hotel, which she did. When I contacted owner Patrick Sheehan and explained that I was interested in investigating the hotel, he was very receptive to the idea. During our phone conversation, he described some of the things he and his girlfriend had experienced on the property.

"One time, my girlfriend and I were standing outside the hotel, near the deck," he explained. *"When I gave her a hug, it sounded like every window in the hotel rattled and shook. It was crazy."*

Patrick told of the time a group came to investigate late one afternoon. They planned to camp out for the night, so he led them to a location on the property where they could set up their tents. *"My girlfriend who was watching us from a distance, later told me that, as I was walking with the group, she saw some type of a black mist or fog following us, then it suddenly disappeared."*

Patrick's girlfriend also witnessed a lady standing on the balcony of the attic. She said the lady was there one minute and then seemed to suddenly fold up and disappear!

The most fascinating story I heard about the hotel was told to me on June 10th, 2010. Patrick asked if I would come down to Morse Mill to be interviewed for the television show, *"The Most Terrifying Places in America,"* due to the EVPs I had recorded during my investigations there. Unfortunately, the film crew never interviewed me due to lack of time. While I was there, I was introduced to a man named Jeff, who told me of an incident that happened to him and two other investigators when they spent the night at the hotel, during an electrical storm.

According to Jeff, his group set up several flashlights on the hotel staircase and were asking the spirits to make the flashlights turn on and off, to verify spirits were present. Jeff said the experiment seemed to be working as the lights would turn on or off as soon as they asked the spirits to manipulate them. As they were doing this, a furious storm came up and a tornado touched down two blocks away.

"We were facing the staircase monitoring the flashlights when a bolt of lightning lit up the room," he said. *"When the lightning lit up the staircase, we couldn't believe our eyes, because we saw a little girl peering at us through the railing of the staircase. When the flash of lightning disappeared, so did the little girl. We never saw her again,"* Jeff said.

I had my own strange experience prior to my investigation of the hotel. Before I investigate a location, I try to arrange a walkthrough days or weeks ahead of the actual investigation in order to see the layout of the building. So, I arranged to meet Patrick, several weeks before the investigation.

It was a hot and muggy July afternoon, so I wore khaki shorts with cargo pockets. When I arrived, I parked my SUV next to the building, and put my keys in the righthand cargo pocket of my shorts. After exchanging greetings, Patrick proceeded to give me a tour of the hotel and surrounding property. After the tour, I returned to my vehicle to retrieve the magazine article that was in the Haunted Times, because Patrick had not seen it. When I opened the door to retrieve the magazine, my eyes inadvertently looked at the vehicle's ignition, which caused me to automatically check my pocket for my keys. When I checked, I panicked because my keys were missing. I stepped out of the vehicle, checked all of my pockets, even turned them inside out and they were gone!

I returned to Patrick, handed him the magazine, and said, *"Patrick, I have lost my car keys."* So, we went back inside the hotel and retraced our footsteps, starting with the basement and ending up in the attic. The keys were nowhere to be found. We headed outside to search the grounds, but I knew that finding the keys in the tall knee-high grass surrounding the hotel would be nearly impossible. Just as we began to look around outside, my right hand brushed the side cargo pocket, causing a jingling sound. When I put my hand in my pocket, I immediately felt my car keys!

The pocket the keys were in was one that I turned inside out earlier, and they were not there. There was no way I could have missed them when I turned the pocket inside out. *"You are not going to believe this, but my keys are in my pocket,"* I yelled to Patrick, who was searching for the keys in the tall grass.

I explained that there was no way I could have missed them, since I had turned the pocket inside out. The keys simply were not there.

Patrick laughed and explained that this type of thing happens all the time at the hotel. He told of how his tools have disappeared even though they were right next to him while working in the building. *"I would search for the tools and later find them right where I left them. The same thing has happened to my keys several times. They mysteriously disappear only to reappear where I left them.*

Other strange things have occurred at Morse Mill. One afternoon, soon after Patrick purchased the hotel, he was working downstairs on the first floor. Patrick a contractor by trade, does most of the restoration work himself. He explained that he stores his tools in a locked room on the second floor. *"I personally installed heavy steel locks and latches that I bolted in the wood doorframes with heavy gage steel screws. One day I was alone in the building, when I heard loud banging and screeching upstairs as if metal was being torn apart. I rushed upstairs and found the door to the tool room open."*

He said the room was locked when he arrived, and not only was the door open, the heavy gauge steel latch was pulled off the door and lying in the center of the hall with the lock still locked and attached to the latch. He had no explanation for how it happened.

While working alone in the building, he has had the overwhelming feeling that a large man is standing behind him. *"It feels like someone follows me around and watches what I am doing,"* he said.

With the experience I had with my disappearing keys, and the stories Patrick told me as well as the other stories I read about, I was anxious to investigate the hotel.

AUGUST 2009 INVESTIGATION

The team I put together for the investigation, consisted of my friend, Jamie Sullivan, paranormal colleague Gary Hawkins, and Dave McCracken, a member of Gary's team from Alton, Illinois.

We met Patrick at 5:00 p.m. and he gave us a key to access the building. Patrick doesn't like to spend a lot of time at the hotel during the evening and rarely if ever goes there after the sun goes down. So, as soon as he gave us the key, he left.

After unloading our equipment, I gave the team a tour of the building. We started with the basement and worked our way up to the attic. The basement is interesting, to say the least. The foundation and walls are made up of limestone. Any paranormal investigator will tell you that if there is paranormal activity at a location, limestone will generally be found on the property.

The basement is divided up into several rooms. One room has a large stone fireplace and is the room that was once used as a speakeasy. To the rear of the room is an old cistern. Patrick, who is a well-respected commercial contractor, told me the cistern is unusual. He explained that its size is unusual with an opening that is twelve feet across. When he started cleaning it out, he found all types of debris in it, including a World War II Army helmet. Patrick said the walls of the cistern were made of fourteen-inch handmade limestone blocks, but once they made their way down past the fifteen-foot level, the blocks were only a few inches thick. Structurally, this didn't make sense to him. One of his theories, was the cistern may have been part of a tunnel entrance for the Underground Railroad, but when he chiseled through the stone wall of the cistern, no tunnel was found. The last time I talked to Patrick, they had made their way down to the eighteen-foot level of the cistern, were still finding debris and had yet to reach the bottom.

At one end of the basement is a small room with a large limestone block in it. There are holes in the block where bolts were once secured. The bolts were used to shackle slaves to keep them from running off. As the story goes, abolitionists brought runaway slaves there to teach them how to read and write before they were moved further north. Some of the slaves didn't speak or understand English and didn't realize the abolitionist were trying to help them and would try to escape if they were not shackled. Many times, when they escaped, they were recaptured and returned to their former masters.

After finishing the walkthrough of the basement, we worked our way up to the attic. The only encounter we had during the night, was with a swarm of wasps in the attic. But after a short road trip to purchase several cans of wasp spray, the problem was solved.

The entire investigation, from 5:00 p.m., until 5:00 a.m. the next morning, was uneventful. However, when we reviewed our audio, we found we had recorded several interesting EVPs, including ones that said, *"Mary Hudson,"* *"Quiet Please,"* *"And I would watch you,"* and one that says, *"Where are you, Henry?"*

The best EVP, however, was what sounded like someone strumming a chord on a guitar, then singing, *"I love you."* It sounded like something you would have heard Jimi Hendrix singing in the 1960s. Despite the EVPs, I was disappointed that we did not have any personal experiences.

AUGUST 2010 INVESTIGATION

One year later, I returned to the Morse Mill Hotel with Craig Whitworth, a paranormal investigator from central Illinois. Even though the hotel seemed to have more of an odd feel to it during the second investigation, once again, there were no personal experiences. We did get high EMF readings on the second floor that seemed to have a pattern to it.

After getting hits on the EMF detector, we noticed if we stood by the doorway of a particular room on the second floor, we would get a spike on the meter. The spike would occur, dissipate then return again. There is no electricity in the hotel, and none of our equipment was causing the spike in EMF readings. At one point during the investigation, the EMF readings moved from room to room. It got to the point we could follow the fluctuation in electromagnetic field readings, in a repeating pattern, from one room to the next, then back again. Plus, the energy was coming from an invisible source.

Later that night, we had another unusual experience in a room on the second floor. The building's owner told me a story about the room during my walkthrough of the hotel the year before. According to Patrick, people who stay overnight in this room are awakened in the middle of the night feeling like they have been touched in inappropriate places. On one particular night, a pair of paranormal investigators, a man and woman, decided to spend the night. After investigating for several hours, they decided to call it a night and get some sleep on a mattress in the room. There was an old electric fan in the room that was not plugged in, since there is no electricity. During the night, the male investigator woke up to the feeling of being touched in a very personal place. Startled, he arose to see who was there. When he looked toward the fan, he could see the electrical cord floating in the air. This scared the investigator and the couple left in the middle of the night.

The night of the 2010 investigation, Patrick showed Craig and I, a small section of the floor that had been cut out by residents of the halfway house, formerly located in the building. It had a hole in it so they could put a finger in the hole to lift up the section of the floor. The compartment was four by twelve inches and was used by the residents to hide drugs. A bed sat over it to conceal its existence.

During our investigation, Craig and I conducted an EVP session in the room and used an EMF detector called a K-II meter as a control device for obtaining answers. Before starting the EVP session, I said out loud, *"If any spirits are present, you can communicate with us by making the lights on the K-II-meter light up. Cause two flashes for yes and three for no."* We began asking questions and it appeared we were getting responses. We started with a control question. The control question I always use is, *"Is Fred Flintstone present in the room?"* Of course, if the light responds with two flashes for "yes," we know it is an electrical anomaly and is not paranormal.

At one point during the EVP session, Craig asked, *"If I find something in the compartment, can I keep it?"* Immediately, the light on the meter began flashing so fast you would have thought we had placed it next to an electrical circuit box. When I played back our audio and video recordings of the incident, a male voice was recorded saying, *"Go shit!"* So, I guess the answer was no!

A bit later, another anomalous event occurred as we came down the stairs. I came down first and Craig followed. He was wearing a special helmet camera that he invented, which is a camera mounted on the back of a construction hardhat. The camera was facing away from him, in order to film the environment behind him. He also carries a handheld camera to record what is in front of him. This special camera setup also records audio. Craig is very innovative in gadgetry, and he has worked in university research in the field of audio, so he is also very good at debunking false EVPs.

As Craig reached the bottom of the staircase, he said, *"Something is causing interference on the handheld camera. I'm getting a rolling picture with lines of interference."*

As soon as he said this, I noticed Craig turn his head and glance behind him. He later told me he thought someone was there. So, basically, he looked back at the same time the interference occurred on his video screen.

A few days later, when we replayed video footage from a camera in the parlor doorway, you can see Craig's head turn and glance up the stairs. To our surprise, the camera also recorded a voice that sounds like a man with a strong east coast accent. The voice simply says, *"Yo, let me,"* as if saying to Craig, *"Let me use the camera."* Even more interesting, you can time Craig turning his head and looking behind him, with the voice speaking. Even though the voice was recorded by several of our cameras and audio recorders, we did not physically hear it.

Also recorded, was an EVP that says, *"Missed your Angels"* or *"Mr. Angels,"* but who or what the voice is referring to is anyone's guess.

The rich history of the hotel alone, makes it worthwhile to visit. It is not every day you visit a place that was a hospital during the Civil War, part of the Underground Railroad, a speakeasy during the Roaring Twenties, frequented by Al Capone and his men, a hotel managed by the country's first female serial killer, and a place with guests like Frank Dalton, Clara Bow, Charlie Chaplin, and Charles Lindberg.

Other than the high EMF readings, I didn't have any personal experiences of the paranormal kind, but you can't ignore recording disembodied voices in a reportedly haunted hotel.

Is something unusual going on at Morse Mill? Based on my disappearing and reappearing keys, unusual EMF activity in a building without electricity and the recording of EVPs, my answer would be yes. Unfortunately, I didn't experience anything as extreme as was reported by the crew that investigated and filmed the Morse Mill Project. I do believe the story Jeff Green told me about seeing the little girl in the flash of lightening, because Jeff was very passionate about what he saw.

So, when you add up all the above, it does seem to point to something unusual going on at the hotel. After all, the definition of paranormal is, *"Beyond the norm,"* and what goes on at the Morse Mill Hotel seems far from normal, so it is definitely a place to put on your bucket list of places to investigate.

SUMMARY

Written in the walls of the places I investigate are stories. When the stories the walls have to tell come alive, I write about what I see and experience. The chapters of the book you have just read, are filled with some of the strange things I have witnessed during my paranormal investigations.

I wish I knew if the sometimes crazy but always remarkable things I have seen in the last twenty-two years of investigating, are glimpses of Heaven, glimpses of a time past, glimpses of the future or possibly a time and place we have not yet been told about or discovered. A place where all things originate, both good and bad and where things we can only imagine, dwell.

A bigger mystery to me is why I have been allowed to see and experience these remarkable and sometimes frightening things. I don't know why I am so drawn to the unexplained nor do I understand why I pursue the things that go bump in the night. But with each tick of the clock on the wall as it counts down my allotted time here on God's green acres, the feeling becomes stronger that someday soon, I'll stop my searching and will be granted answers to finally understand the why part of the equation.

But until that day, I will continue working on the mystery that is the paranormal, searching for answers, pursuing the unexplained.

Happy Hauntings

Larry Wilson

About the Author

Larry Wilson spent a decade working as a private investigator, before turning his attention to the paranormal. He is the founder of Urban Paranormal Investigations in central Illinois. In addition to investigating hundreds of locations throughout the Midwest, he is a "Best Selling Author" who has written several books on the topic, guest lecturer and has appeared on both television and radio programs.

Larry has assisted in the filming of four paranormal documentaries for independent film companies and can be heard on, "The Paranormal Pursuit" podcast on all major media platforms.

Wilson currently resides in Taylorville, Illinois with his wife Kathy and son Cory.

Like us on Facebook:
https://www.facebook.com/Urban-Paranormal-Investigations-327088597440791/

Photo by Kathy Wilson

Books by Larry Wilson

Chasing Shadows
Echoes from the Grave
Dark Creepy Places
Where Evil Lurks
Dr. Ugs – A Haunting in Virginia, Illinois
Paranormal Road Trip
Strange Williamsburg Hill
Things That Go Bump in the Night